BOOK OF SECRETS

BOOK OF SECRETS

**Andrews McMeel
Publishing, LLC**

Kansas City

BOOK OF SECRETS

For information, write Andrews McMeel Publishing, LLC, an Andrews McMeel Universal
company, 1130 Walnut Street, Kansas City, Missouri 64106.

10 11 12 WKT 10 9 8 7

ISBN-13: 978-0-7407-7754-7
ISBN-10: 0-7407-7754-8

Library of Congress Control Number: 2008921154

www.andrewsmcmeel.com

Produced by Essential Works
168a Camden Street, London NW1 9PT, England

Designed by Kate Ward for Essential Works

Images of abandoned New York subway stations courtesy of Joseph Brennan

ATTENTION: SCHOOLS AND BUSINESSES

Andrews McMeel books are available at quantity discounts with bulk purchase
for educational, business, or sales promotional use. For information, please write to:
Special Sales Department, Andrews McMeel Publishing, LLC, 1130 Walnut Street,
Kansas City, Missouri 64106.

INTRODUCTION

KNOWLEDGE IS POWER

Of course, power corrupts, but who doesn't want to be corrupted a little?

Who doesn't want to know as much as possible about everything and anything? Clearly you do, or you wouldn't be reading this book. It's a strange thing, but the world is becoming ever more public, in as much as there are cameras watching our every move, and electronic tracking devices that can pinpoint what we have spent where and when. The notion of "private lives" is a quaint anachronism, and yet the world is still full of secrets. Those secrets can be big or small, white or very dark, but they are all the currency of people who like to deal in knowledge. Or rather, hold back their secret knowledge because it can make them richer—monetarily or spiritually. In an age when man is constantly bombarded with information from all manner of media, including 24-hour news broadcasts, Internet streaming, and mobile telecommunications technology, that secrets exist is in itself an amazing fact.

The quest to uncover secrets has driven men to madness and great feats of discovery; it has brought them to ruin and great riches—Colonel Sanders, for instance, would never have created the KFC empire without the secret element in his Southern fried chicken. Similarly, Coca-Cola would be just another soft drink without its secret ingredient. Then there are the world's secret services, who have made and prevented wars by their very secret activities.

This book is too small to contain all of the secrets of the world, of course. Any book would be too small, but it does contain an incredible array of secrets, from an impressive range of subject areas. There are food secrets, secret buildings, secrets of the rich and famous, secrets of success and of human relationships, plus many more. You can dip in and out and absorb the secrets contained within these pages, and so feel a little wiser and a little more knowledgeable. Go on, corrupt yourself a little.

X (editor)

THE SECRET OF ATTRACTING BEAUTIFUL WOMEN

According to legend, Freud's dying words were: "What do women want?" Thankfully for men, post-Freud teachings have produced a glut of soul-searching self-help books that reveal just that. In no particular order, here are the top ten things women secretly look for in a man.

1. BE APPEALING

After first impressions have faded, women are more attracted to a man's manner than his look. A man should therefore work on honing his charm and becoming more appealing. Looks aren't everything.

2. LEAD AN INTERESTING LIFE

A recent survey revealed that, more than anything else, women look for a man who has led an interesting life, citing their ideal men as Bill Clinton, Sting, and even Prince Charles. So don't refer to your failed business venture; instead, spin the truth to make the episode sound like yet another example of your brave, impetuous, go-getting nature.

3. AIM HIGHER

Beautiful women frequently complain that men never approach them. This is because male pride doesn't take well to rejection. But if you become the kind of man who can approach these women, you may be surprised by the success you have. Remember: Men who are successful with women are merely those who have experienced more rejection.

4. DRESS WELL

Women like a man who is well-groomed and tidy. Or, in other words, one who is presentable in public. But don't spend too much time on your appearance—a woman will rarely date a man who is prettier than she is.

5. MAKE HER LAUGH

Woody Allen often jokes that he has never laughed a woman into bed, yet he has been surprisingly successful with women. Plus, a GSOH (Good Sense Of Humor) is still the most popular phrase in personal ads. A woman will find humor entertaining, of course, and a sure-fire guarantee of no awkward silences on a date. This subconsciously means that she can relax and be the passenger, not the driver.

6. BE SINCERE

Women are receptive to men who are kind, thoughtful, sincere, and good listeners.

7. BUT DON'T BE TOO SINCERE

Another study revealed that women instinctively divide men into those they consider friends and those who have the potential to become lovers. The sweet man will only ever be the friend.

8. PLAY CAT AND MOUSE

If she's playing hard to get, then do the same—over-eager men, like over-eager women, can appear desperate. But you must make the next move. A woman never wants to feel like the predator.

9. MAKE HER FEEL SPECIAL

Treat her as if she's unique, unlike anyone else you have ever met. Appreciate her and never take her for granted.

10. DO YOUR HOMEWORK

Find out what her father is like—for most women, he will be the first and most powerful image of manhood. Then determine what you want: Women want a fling with a cad but a relationship with a dad. Manipulate your game plan accordingly.

ABANDONED NEW YORK SUBWAY STATIONS #1

CITY HALL

LOCATION: UNDER CITY HALL PARK

OPENED IN OCTOBER 1904, CLOSED DECEMBER 1945.

It was the original southern terminal of the Interborough Rapid Transit (IRT) subway and designed to be the showpiece of the new subway. Unusually elegant in architectural style, it is unique among the original IRT stations in that the platform and mezzanine feature Guastavino arches and skylights, colored glass tilework, and brass chandeliers. Because its platform is short and very tightly curved, when increased ridership of the subway required that original five-car local stations be lengthened to accommodate longer trains, it was abandoned in favor of the nearby Brooklyn Bridge station. While very few people have actually seen City Hall Station, the #6 train still passes through it on its way north, reversing direction using the loop for the journey back to the Bronx. On the surface, all that can be seen of the station is a concrete slab inset with glass tiles, which are the skylights for the platform below. This patch of concrete is in the middle of a grove of dogwoods in front of City Hall, close to Broadway. Recent security measures at City Hall have closed the area to visitors. ✐

THE SECRET TO SURVIVING A SHARK ATTACK

The best way to survive the attack of a shark is to avoid it. So don't swim in any waters where sharks are likely to also swim and certainly don't swim where there's low visibility and/or no lifeguard on duty. Also remember that sharks feed at night.

If you must swim where sharks are known to exist, don't swim alone. Do not wear bright colors in the water. The kind of food that sharks are attracted to tends to be silver, white, or yellow, so don't wear jewelry either, since that can have the same reflective effect and attract sharks. Don't swim in commercial fishing areas. If you spot shoals of small, silver fish in the water, there are likely to be sharks watching the same shoal. Likewise, the presence of birds in the water or swooping into it is a sign that the shark's favorite food is around. Sharks have a highly developed sense of smell and can detect blood and waste matter from miles away. Don't swim if you're bleeding, and definitely do not pass body waste into the water. Even if you spot a shark nearby, control your bodily functions.

If you are attacked by a shark, make a lot of noise and splash heavily. Some authorities recommend shouting under water. Despite what you might think, lying "dead" in the water will attract a shark to bite you. Swim fast and messily and change direction suddenly— sharks are like tankers in that they can't change direction as quickly as they'd like (which is why dolphins often get the better of them). If you're with people, bunch together and all kick or punch at the approaching shark. If you have a knife on you, aim it at the shark's eyes or gills. Of course, because none of us ever has the sharp knife we need when we need it, you can punch or gouge at the shark's eyes—that is, if you have the nerve to face it. Swimming away from the shark is the best course of action, even if you've been bitten.

Whatever happens, keep moving, make noise, and try to attract the attention of others—and never, ever, give up.

A PRESIDENT SPEAKS ON SECRETS

"THE VERY WORD 'SECRECY' IS REPUGNANT IN A FREE AND
OPEN SOCIETY; AND WE ARE AS A PEOPLE INHERENTLY AND
HISTORICALLY OPPOSED TO SECRET SOCIETIES, TO SECRET
OATHS, AND TO SECRET PROCEEDINGS."
John F. Kennedy (*member of the Ancient Order of Hibernians
1947–1963, U.S. president 1961–1963*)

LITTLE KNOWN CULINARY CURIOS #1

Freshly killed chickens will always have more flavor. They can be bought at kosher shops.

It takes almost 11 pounds of grapes to produce 2 pounds of raisins, sultanas, or currants.

Stir a teaspoon of cornflour mixed into a paste with water into yogurt before adding to a sauce as a healthy substitute for cream. It will stop it separating when it gets hot.

Adding salt to dried beans' cooking water will toughen the bean skins. 🖫

THE SECRETS OF GIVING FLOWERS #1

In the restrained, subtle Victorian era, when actions spoke louder than words and much was left unsaid, seduction was highly codified and the giving of flowers was particularly symbolic. The giving of flowers is a much more complicated business than one might think. The various meanings of individual flowers are not always favorable or even consistent with each other, and there are secret messages to be found in how they are presented:

With blooms facing upward
my message is favorable

With blooms facing downward
my message is unfavorable

Flowers given with
the right hand
I agree

Flowers given with
the left hand
I disagree

Kissing a received flower
yes

Plucking or discarding a petal
no ☒

SECRETS OF YOUR COMPUTER KEYBOARD

AOL's keyboard grime analysis established that the major constituents of a London office's keyboard dirt are as follows:

Corn Flakes	15%	Staple	1%
Hard candy	15%	Finger nail	1%
Noodles	7%	Tape/plastic	1%
Vegetable piece	4%	Insect	1%
Leaf	1%	Foil	1%
Pencil lead/shavings	1%	Hair	1%

⏳

THE SECRET BERLIN TUNNEL

During the Cold War, Berlin held many secrets and the Altglienicke district of the city was the site of one of the most audacious intelligence coups of the era. Starting in 1954, a 500-meter tunnel was constructed from West to East Berlin in order to intercept landlines used by Soviet military and intelligence. Unknown to the CIA, however, the entire operation had been compromised by a British mole, George Blake. The construction of the tunnel was allowed to continue though, as his handler didn't want to run the risk of exposing their star agent. Initially, the KGB kept knowledge of the tunnel from the GRU (Soviet Military Intelligence) and their East German allies. The tunnel was eventually "accidentally" discovered in April 1956, but not before the operation had produced some 50,000 reels of magnetic tapes of Soviet and East German telephone and teletype traffic. The western intelligence agencies were still interpreting this information more than two years after the closure of the tunnel.

This was not the only Cold War–era tunnel dug in Berlin, though. On 14 September 1962, 29 people fled under the Berlin Wall through a mile-long tunnel that ran from an East German cellar into the Western zone. Flooding shortly afterward prevented any others from using the same method of escape. ⌀

THE SORCERER WHO INSPIRED HARRY POTTER

From where does J. K. Rowling get her inspiration? History, it seems. The character of the sorcerer Nicolas Flamel, who appeared in the book *Harry Potter and the Sorcerer's Stone*, was based on a real medieval Parisian bookseller and alchemist. Born around 1330, Flamel spent much of his life searching for the "philosopher's stone," the substance that would turn base metals into gold and produce the elixir of life. After a premonition in a dream, he purchased a manuscript, *The Book of Abraham the Jew*, which he claimed contained the secrets of alchemy. The house in which Flamel lived at 51 Rue Montmorency in Paris is now a restaurant. ↶

SECRETS OF THE HOUSE

1   A casino speeds up the game if they are worried about losing money. On average, the more games played, the higher their percentage.

2   Are all the players genuine? People from outside and even security guards may be asked to play to make a casino look fuller.

3   Casinos want you to lose touch with the outside world and your sense of time. There are no clocks inside a casino, dealers do not wear watches, and often there are no windows.

4   Don't be pleasantly surprised by all the free drinks on offer in a casino. It's a business. They want to keep you there and the more drunk you are the less you're likely to win.

5   In a busy game, watch out for the guy who is prepared to steal chips from someone else's pile. ⧖

THE SECRET OF THE BLACK BOX?

Everyone knows that Black Box Flight Recorders aren't black—they're orange so as to be as conspicuous as possible. So why is it called that? Because the first version of the in-flight recorder was invented by a man named Black.

While originally they recorded everything that was said in the cabin, now they also keep a video record and monitor all the plane's operational systems. 🖫

UNDERGROUND SECRETS OF NEW YORK

In the 1980s a very secret, underground society sprang up under the Big Apple's streets, fuelled by poverty, homelessness, and drug addiction. The so-called Molemen lived in the vast network of tunnels beneath the city, with the total numbers estimated between 1,000 and 5,000. Many congregated in the area underneath Grand Central Station. Lurid reports were told of mutants or Chuds (Cannibalistic Humanoid Underground Dwellers), but the truth was sadder and more prosaic. Today, due to tougher law enforcement and outreach programs, there are fewer of them, but the secret Molemen of New York still exist. ᖆ

HOW THE KGB PASSED SECRETS IN THE WEST

The Russians always demonstrated a sense of humor when it came to espionage and operations on enemy soil. Since they were firmly against both organized religion and the trappings of capitalist success, KGB spymasters obviously thought that it would be amusing—and perhaps less suspicious—if they used churches in wealthy London areas for some of their dirty work. During the Cold War, the KGB operated two "dead letter drops" where agents left secret material to be picked up by their handlers in Kensington. One was behind two pillars near the Pieta statue in Brompton Oratory, a Catholic Church on the Brompton Road. Another was in the yard of Holy Trinity Church in Cottage Place, where packages were left by the tree beside a statue of St. Francis of Assisi. ᘓ

SECRET TRICKS OF THE TRADE

ACTOR

A wise older actor once told Michael Caine, "don't act like a drunk man. Act like a drunk man trying hard to be sober."

GRAPHIC DESIGNER

To pacify the client who thinks they are a designer and cannot pass anything without making their mark, give your design an obvious mistake: a huge logo or dumb font. The client will correct that and your design will go through as it should.

BALLOON TWISTER

Don't specify in advance what animal you're making—you're setting yourself up for failure. Ask children afterward what it looks like to them. Rely on their imagination.

MAKE-UP ARTIST

Applying a thin line of concealer around the outside edge of the lips gives them more definition. Dabbing lipgloss along the length of cheekbones makes them more prominent.

HAIRDRESSER

Watch your hairdresser's facial twitches and shoulder hunches in the mirror. Hairdressers utilize the complicated arrangements of mirrors in their salon to convey to each other urgent judgments about their clients. ⧗

THE SECRET HISTORY OF KOTEX

Many technological innovations are developed during wartime. In 1914, the paper supplier Kimberly-Clark developed a new type of material out of processed wood and called it Cellucotton. It was half as cheap to produce as cotton and five times more absorbent. In a patriotic gesture it was soon being sold to the War Department at cost, and used to dress wounds in World War I.

When the war was over, the company had to find another use for its product. Until then, women had been using rags for sanitary protection, but someone came up with the idea of using Cellucotton for the same purpose. Their marketing agency suggested the name Kotex, an abbreviation of "cotton textile," and a whole new era of disposable sanitary products began.

In 1928, Lee Miller's image was one of the first to be used in a Kotex advertisement—to her initial chagrin, and later pride. Then magazines and retail outlets underwent a similar change of heart. To start with neither would take the products, but by 1935 Tampax had come on to the market and by 1945, American women were almost exclusively using commercially produced sanitary napkins and tampons. ⧖

THE SECRET TO SURVIVING SNAKE BITE

A lot of people get bitten by snakes in America—up to 50,000 a year, in fact. The secret to surviving a snake bite is primarily not to panic. Only a fifth of bites come from poisonous snakes and a ridiculously low number ever result in death (about 15 a year). So STAY CALM.

If bitten, sit still for half an hour or so. Any movement speeds up your blood flow (as does panicking, remember) and you don't want that. Get into a position that keeps the bitten area below heart level. Now remove anything that can impede blood flow, including rings, which will prevent the bite area from swelling. If the area of the bite begins to swell and change color, the snake was probably poisonous. That might put you into shock, so make sure that you're comfortable and able to keep warm.

If your bite is on a hand, finger, foot, or toe, wrap your leg or arm with a bandage (rip it from your clothes if necessary) and tie it between the bite and your heart, kind of like those ties that nurses put on when you're having a blood test. Try to leave any fang marks open to the air and make sure that the bandage allows flow of blood, only restricted.

Despite what you might have seen in the movies, do not either cut into the bite nor attempt to suck out the poison. And even if you could, don't put an ice pack or similar aide on the bite since that can make it worse.

Remain calm and after your half-hour rest, walk steadily and at a not-too-fast pace to the nearest emergency room.

THE SECRET OF KEEPING BABIES QUIET

A reliable remedy for colic in babies is a teaspoon of onion water. Make an infusion by steeping a roughly chopped onion in hot water then leaving it to cool. This can be kept in a sealed jar, in the fridge, for three or four days. 🖫

ABANDONED NEW YORK SUBWAY STATIONS #2

COURT STREET

LOCATION: COURT STREET AT BOERUM PLACE AND

SCHERMERHORN STREET

OPENED IN APRIL 1936, CLOSED JUNE 1946.

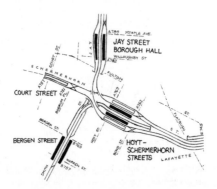

Because it is so close to stations with direct service to Manhattan, it never had much ridership. Its closure also eliminated any use for outer platforms at the nearby Hoyt-Schermerhorn Sts. Though almost unused for thirty years, in the 1960s it became a subway station set for movies, and an entrance at Boerum Place was re-opened. It was perfect because trains could be put in it, and moved in and out as required for movie scenes, with no interference at all to regular train service. As part of their Bicentennial celebrations in 1976, the Transit Authority set up what was called the New York City Transit Exhibit at Court Street, which opened on July 4. Admission was one subway token. Although billed as temporary, it has continued to the present day, and is now known as the New York Transit Museum. Special Nostalgia Train tours operate in and out of the station a few times a year. ᐧ

THE SECRET LANGUAGE OF CODE TALKERS

One of the stranger episodes in the secret history of cryptology was the use of Navajo speakers in the Second World War. The

U.S. military, concerned over Japanese success in deciphering their codes, recruited a group of young Navajos and asked them to devise their own code. Everyday Navajo words were used to represent a military vocabulary—ships were named after fish, bombs were eggs, and tanks were turtles. The Navajos found it ironic that their language was being enlisted for the service of the nation. At school, they had often been punished for speaking it. The code could be quickly transmitted and was never broken by the Japanese. The finest hour of the code talkers was at the bloody capture of Iwo Jima, where six Navajos transmitted more than 800 faultless messages. ᘐ

THE SECRET OF GETTING RICE RIGHT #1

Wild rice isn't rice at all, but derives from a grass grown in water.

Wild rice is far more nutritious than the regular variety: It is rich in all eight amino acids, is much higher in fiber, and lower in calories, and has hardly any gluten content.

You can reduce the cooking time of wild rice—about 60 minutes, twice that of regular rice—by soaking it overnight.

Stop rice sticking together by washing it under cold running water until the water runs clear before you start boiling it. This gets rid of the excess starch that causes the stickiness.

Do not stir rice while you are cooking it as this will release starch from the grains, which will stick them together.

Brown rice will take longer to cook than white rice—about 10 minutes longer—but brown rice will be chewier when cooked, so don't be tempted to overcook it thinking it isn't quite done yet. 🖫

99 LBS. NET WEIGHT

WHOLE BEAN
UNCOATED

TABLE RICE

THE SECRET FLIGHT TO CUBA

In spite of the official boycott, there is one commercial flight a day between Miami International and Havana, Cuba. However, there's no point in looking for details about the flight and certainly no way that you could book yourself onto it. The daily flight to Cuba does not appear on any information boards or publicly available schedules, and the only Americans permitted to fly on it are members of the press and media services.

If you do manage to wangle a trip on the flight—maybe you could get a writing assignment for your local newspaper?—do not expect to be able to prove to friends that you'd actually made the trip. On arrival in the socialist republic, instead of having their passports stamped with incriminating evidence of having been in the land of hand-rolled cigars, an entry visa is stamped on a square of paper and attached to the visiting journalist's passport with a paper clip. So there is no indelible record of the traveler having visited the island. And any cigars brought back are likely to be confiscated, of course.

All of which is historically bizarre, since the first international commercial passenger flight to depart America, in 1920, was to Cuba from South Florida. ▣

THE SECRET GRAVE AT KING'S CROSS STATION

King's Cross Station in London may now be best known as the hidden departure point for the Hogwarts Express, the train Harry Potter takes to school from Platform 9 and three-quarters. But according to legend, it is also the secret burial site of the ancient British warrior Queen Boudicca, who is buried nearby under Platform 10. In A.D. 60, after the death of her husband Prasutagus, king of the Iceni, and the brutalization of her family, she led a savage rebellion against Roman rule. After burning Colchester and St. Albans, she marched on London, but her forces were finally defeated at the site of King's Cross station. The area used to be known as Battle Bridge, and Roman military equipment has been uncovered during construction work. Once defeat was inevitable, Boudicca and her daughters are said to have taken poison rather than be tortured and publicly humiliated by her Roman conquerors, and they were buried on the battlefield. ᗱ

SECRET PARISIAN CINEMA FOUND

In September of 2004, police found a cinema-cum-restaurant in a cavern under the French capital's 16th arrondissement. When asked who built it and why, the authorities shook their head and shrugged in a Gallic kind of way.

"We have no idea whatsoever," said a police spokesman. "There were two swastikas painted on the ceiling, but also celtic crosses and several stars of David, so we don't think it's extremists. Some sect or secret society, maybe." With that uniquely French air of insouciance the spokesman shrugged and finished with the line,

"There are any number of possibilities."

There are 170 miles of tunnels, caves, galleries, and catacombs underneath Paris. The police stumbled on the cinema while on a training exercise across the Seine from the Eiffel Tower, under the Palais de Chaillot. Entering through a drain next to the Trocadero, they were confronted by a tarpaulin marked "Building Site, No Access," behind which was a desk and CCTV set to record anyone who entered (and triggered a tape of dogs barking).

Farther down, the tunnel opened out into a vast

cave—like an underground amphitheater—around 54 feet underground. Here they found projection equipment, a screen, and tapes of a wide variety of films including 1950s film noir classics and more recent thrillers. There was nothing subversive, illegal, or offensive about their content.

An adjacent smaller cave contained a restaurant and bar. "There were bottles of whisky and other spirits . . . tables and chairs, a pressure-cooker for making couscous," the spokesman went on, barely concealing his admiration for the organization. "The whole thing ran off a professionally installed electricity system and there were at least three phone lines."

But when they returned with experts from the French electricity board three days later, the phone and electricity lines had been cut. "Do not," read a note left lying in the middle of the cavern floor, "try to find us."

Within days a group called the Perforating Mexicans claimed on French radio that the underground cinema was its work. Patrick Alk, author of a book on the urban underground exploration movement, said the discovery was "a shame but not the end of the world." There were, he said, "a dozen more where that one came from." ⌛

SYSTEMS OF FOREIGN ELECTRONIC SURVEILLANCE IN THE U.S.

A professional in the field of technical surveillance countermeasure (TSCM) revealed the following about the U.S. government's tolerance of diplomatic electronic spying in the U.S., including the United Nations (notwithstanding international treaty and U.S. law prohibiting such spying), in 2003:

1   Britain, Canada, and Australia have greater latitude than other countries for electronic spying in the U.S.

2   Foreign governments can electronically spy on one another in the U.S. but not on U.S. citizens.

3   Electronic spying can be done only from diplomatically exempt locations, i.e., office, home, or vehicle.

4   Electronic spying can be done only by government officials, not private contractors hired for the purpose.

5   Private contractors are not likely to have as sophisticated equipment as governments and will almost certainly be detected by governmental targets and/or USG TSCM units.

6 Governments locate their premises to have line-of-sight of targets and to be nearby.

7 Orientation of visible antennae on government premises can indicate targets. ✍

THE SECRET OF HAPPINESS

"THE SECRET OF HAPPINESS IS THIS: LET YOUR INTERESTS BE AS WIDE AS POSSIBLE, AND LET YOUR REACTIONS TO THE THINGS AND PERSONS THAT INTEREST YOU BE AS FAR AS POSSIBLE FRIENDLY RATHER THAN HOSTILE."
Bertrand Russell (*20th-century British philosopher*)

"THE SECRET OF HAPPINESS IS SOMETHING TO DO."
John Burroughs (*19th-century American author*)

THE SECRET OF A GOOD CUP OF COFFEE

Vietnam is the second biggest coffee producer in the world, after Brazil. This is in spite of the climate being unsuitable and the industry over-reliant on chemical fertilizers as they rotate crops too quickly, and, as a result, Vietnamese coffee is inferior. It is also cheaper, and therefore used to make instant coffee or to bulk up blends of better-quality beans.

When coffee is brewed and dried to become instant granules, the process will destroy much of the natural aroma. It is therefore reintroduced to what reaches the consumer in the form of aromatic oils that react with the air once the jar's seal is broken.

Increased mechanization in coffee harvesting may be contributing to cancer. When coffee "cherries" (the fruit that is roasted to become the "bean") are picked by hand, the immature green fruit is left on the tree. Mechanized picking removes whole clusters of cherries and cannot differentiate between ripe and underripe. As there is no, or very little, hand sorting or checking, these green cherries get into the roasting system and are roasted into black beans that not only impair the grounds' flavor but are susceptible to a cancer-causing fungus. 🖫

THE SECRET OF BARGAIN HUNTING (CLOTHES)

Find a flaw. Point out the fault to the staff—you should get a discount of around 10 percent, depending on the damage. This is even more likely if you're a popular size (they'll have sold out of alternatives) or an odd size (they'll only have one sample in stock).

Only shop on a Thursday. That's when the majority of stores get their new stock delivered. Get there early and bag the best bargains.

Become skinny. A size six is a sample size designed to fit models. Most designers sell clothes worn on the catwalk or in showrooms at vastly discounted prices. Look for ads for sample sales in most city newspapers.

Only shop during the sales. And only on the first or last day. Best buys will have vanished after day one, but by the end the remainder will have been slashed to bargain-basement prices. Save time by visiting the store before the sale to decide what you want. ❀

LITTLE KNOWN CULINARY CURIOS #2

The most reliable way to make a lumpy sauce is to attempt to mix flour and hot liquid together directly—the flour will start cooking immediately. Mix the flour with fat—not oil—first and cook the two together to form a "roux."

Once the grains of the flour have started to open up the liquid will combine smoothly.

The secret to re-baking a cold baked potato is to dip it in water and give it 15 minutes in a very hot oven.

Cakes collapse if you open the oven door because heat expands air bubbles in the cake and makes it rise. A sudden rush of cold air reverses the process.

If you are steaming vegetables or fish, salt added to the water you are boiling will raise the temperature and cook your food more quickly.

THE SECRET OF BARGAIN HUNTING (TRAVEL)

Plan carefully. Many business hotels offer reduced prices at weekends; similarly, many tourist hotels and packages are cheaper out of season.

Become an air courier. This is someone who carries documents for a courier company on international flights. They get discounted flights, so this is a great way to see the world at a bargain price. Approach individual courier companies for more details.

Shop around. Despite the deceptive name, no-frills airlines do not always offer the cheapest deals. With a little time and use of the Internet you can root out the real bargains.

Become a vulture tourist. Travel to countries with unstable economies or former war-torn nations that have recently been removed from the official, state-issued no-go list. Yes, it's ruthless, but this way you are guaranteed the best bargains—plus you will be helping their economy. ✿

THE SECRET FIRST SCREENING OF *STAR WARS*

The film that we now know as the tenth most successful of all time had a very, very bad beginning. Once upon a very long time ago, at a private screening, George Lucas previewed his follow-up to *American Graffiti* to fellow directors Steven Spielberg, Francis Ford Coppola, Martin Scorsese, and Brian de Palma.

The film he unveiled was a rough cut of *Star Wars*. There wasn't any music, whole chunks of the plot were missing, and the galactic battle scenes hadn't been completed, so Lucas used stock footage of WWII dogfights to fill in. But the omens were not good—de Palma took Lucas to one side to commiserate. Indeed, no one, save Spielberg, thought that there was really any future in Lucas's futuristic adventure. Even the actors joined in: On being shown a rough draft of the script, Harrison Ford told the writer/director, "George, you can type this shit, but you sure can't say it!"

But Lucas was soon vindicated. On its release in 1977, *Star Wars* was an immediate hit and it went on to become the most successful film of all time, a title it held until it was overtaken five years later by *ET*, directed by none other than Steven Spielberg. ⌂

ABANDONED NEW YORK SUBWAY STATIONS #3

HOYT-SCHERMERHORN STREETS

LOCATION: AT HOYT, SCHERMERHORN, AND BOND STREETS
OPENED IN APRIL 1936, CLOSED JUNE 1946. RE-OPENED IN
SEPTEMBER 1959, CLOSED MARCH 1981.

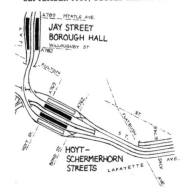

Like Court Street, this station was part of an independent subway system built by the Board of Transportation. Originally closed in 1946 along with Court Street, Hoyt-Schermerhorn Sts. was used again from 1959 to 1981 for Aqueduct Racetrack special trains, since it was the only stop between 42 St. at 8 Ave. and the track. It is now sometimes used as a movie set as was formerly done at Court St. ᴖ

ELVIS'S SECRET RECORDING

The world knows and loves Elvis's hits—from "That's All Right (Mama)" to "Way Down," the King sold millions of records. But there's one recording that has never been mentioned in anyone's list of their favorite Elvis recordings. "You can get 'em piping hot, after 4pm; you can get 'em piping hot. Southern Maid Doughnuts hit the spot . . ." were the lyrics to perhaps not the most exciting advertising jingle ever, but it was the only one that Elvis Presley ever sang.

On 6 November 1954, the 19-year-old was fourth on the bill at the Louisiana Hayride and like a lot of other performers on the show, Elvis sang the praises of the show's sponsors, Southern Maid Doughnuts. He may not have made much money, but the teenager sure got a lot of complimentary doughnuts. ⌂

THE SECRET OF SAN DIEGO'S WGASA LINE

In the San Diego Wild Animal Park, a monorail runs around a huge enclosure, allowing visitors to observe the animals within. It is known as the Wgasa line. Why Wgasa? In 1972 busy staff at the new park were struggling to think of a name for the monorail when the chief designer suggested a then well-known acronym that reflected both their struggle and their attitude toward it. The name stuck and spread so quickly that it was kept. The acronym stood for "Who Gives a Shit Anyway?" ⧗

THE SECRET TO STACKING BREAD

Each loaf of bread sold in a supermarket has a colored twist tie around it that serves a dual purpose. Not only does it keep the bread in the bag but it tells the shelf stacker how fresh it is. Each day of the week is assigned a color, presumably allowing the stacker to ensure that the oldest loaves are placed in the most prominent position. As a customer, one might not know the store or company's code without asking, but if there are loaves of bread with three different colors of twist tie on a shelf they deserve closer inspection of the "Best Before Date" since one of them is to be avoided. Even if there are two colors, armed with this information, it is possible to identify the freshest. ⧖

THE SECRET HISTORY OF THE TOWER OF LONDON

The Tower of London has a fearsome reputation as the scene of bloody persecution, imprisonment, and violent death. It's true that in the Tudor years many royal and political opponents from Anne Boleyn to Lady Jane Grey, and Thomas More to Thomas Cromwell were executed there by royal decree. What's less known is that for a period of over 150 years—since the beheading of the Scottish Jacobite Simon 11th Lord Lovat on 9 April 1747—no executions took place in the Tower. Until, that is, the First World War, when 11 Germans convicted of espionage were shot there. The last execution took place during the Second World War in 1941, when Josef Jakobs, a German who had been convicted of spying, was strapped to a chair and shot by firing squad. Ironically, the last person to die in the Tower was visitor Dorothy Household in 1974. She was killed when a bomb, thought to be planted by the IRA, went off in the White Tower. ᐧᕹ

THE SECRET OF MY SUCCESS

"EIGHTY PERCENT OF SUCCESS IS SHOWING UP."
Woody Allen (*20th-century American comedian*)

"I DON'T KNOW THE KEY TO SUCCESS, BUT THE KEY TO
FAILURE IS TRYING TO PLEASE EVERYBODY."
Bill Cosby (*20th-century American comedian*)

SECRET CHRISTIAN CATACOMBS

The ancient Romans cremated their dead and forbade burials of bodies within the city limits. The early Christians dug out over 200 miles of tunnels outside the city of Rome and used recesses within the passageways as tombs, and as a place where they could practice their faith unmolested. The catacombs now provide the earliest example of Christian art in the remaining sculptures, sarcophagi, frescoes, and inscriptions. One recurring theme in this artwork is the Christian "fish"—still used today on U.S. cars and business cards to identify those who follow the Christian faith. The fish was an important ancient symbol of Christianity, used in parables such as that of the loaves and fishes. But the Greek word for fish—"ICHTHYS"—was also used as a religious acrostic by the early Christians as a credo to express their faith and as a secret means to identify each other. The Greek letter "I" referred to Jesus, or "Iesus" as he was then known; the "CH" to Christos or Christ; the "TH" to Theou or God; the "Y" to Yios or son; and the "S" to Soter or savior. The meaning is "Jesus Christ God Son Savior." ✐

THE SECRET READING LIST

FIVE BOOKS THAT HAVE TO BE READ IN SECRET IN SOME PARTS OF AMERICA:

THE *JOY OF SEX*, AND *MORE JOY OF SEX* BY ALEX COMFORT

In 1978, these books were banned by Lexington, Kentucky, police in accordance with a new county law prohibiting the display of sexually orientated publications in places frequented by minors.

THE ADVENTURES OF HUCKLEBERRY FINN
BY MARK TWAIN

The world "nigger" appears throughout this book. In 1984, it was removed from an eighth-grade reading list in Waukegan, Illinois, because an alderman found it offensive. In the fall of 2003, the Renton School District removed it from their approved reading list.

AS I LAY DYING BY WILLIAM FAULKNER

In 1986, the school board at Graves County, Kentucky—none of whom, it is alleged, had read the book—banned this from its high school English reading list. They banned it because it contained seven passages that referred to God or abortion, and included words such as "bastard," "goddam," and "son of a bitch."

SNOW FALLING ON CEDARS BY DAVID GUTERSON

In 2000, after a community debate, it was decided by the South

Kitsap County School District board that this award-winning book should be removed from the reading list, allegedly due to its sexual content, language, and promotion of intolerance.

THE *HARRY POTTER* SERIES BY J. K. ROWLING

In 2003, a church group from Greenville, Michigan, burned this series on the basis that it concerned itself with the dark arts. The group felt it should be made known that the books were about witchcraft. ⌛

FOOD STUFF THEY'D RATHER YOU DIDN'T KNOW #1

Modified Atmosphere Packaging (MAP) is the "air" that surrounds the leaves in sealed bags of pre-packed salad, and it will have an increased carbon dioxide content at the expense of oxygen. While this is what stops the salad leaves from wilting and discoloring for anything up to a month, it will greatly reduce the leaves' vitamin C and E content.

Health authorities recommend washing pre-packed salad before eating it, even though it is sold as being already washed, because there is a very high probability of it being washed in a strong chlorine solution.

Ginko and ginseng may do wonders for concentration, but by stimulating blood flow to the brain they can also contribute to or trigger migraines and headaches. If you are a migraine sufferer it is wisest to stay away from such herbal supplements.

The incidents of fruit- or vegetable-related food poisoning have more than doubled in the last decade, with salmonella and E. coli being the front-runners.

Blended cooking oils should be avoided, as they will contain palm or coconut oil, which are both relatively very high in saturated fats.

It is estimated that, on or in their food, the average adult consumes over two gallons of pesticide a year. Carefully wash any fruit or vegetable that is not going to be peeled.

Coffee beans lose most of their flavor during the decaffeination process, and it has to be reintroduced artificially. 🖫

SECRETS OF AIR TRAVEL

There are numerous entertaining urban myths surrounding the matter of air travel. This is probably because the business of flying is opaque at the best of times. Take the matter of getting an upgrade, for instance. Never mind wearing a suit or flashing a smile, "free" upgrades to business class or first class are based on one thing only: how much you paid for your ticket. If the flight can sell more business class seats than it has available, passengers who have paid full fare (or nearest to it) will be bumped up to create extra seats at the back.

Why the price of airline tickets for the same journey can vary from day to day, or even from minute to minute, is because the airline's central computer is perpetually calculating how much that flight needs to earn to make the required profit, and will readjust the fares after each ticket is sold.

Overbooking is policy on every airline except those based in Japan. Taking reservations for more passengers than the aircraft will hold is to ensure the flight is still full after the usual number of "no shows" (on average 2 percent of every flight) have been accounted for. Japanese airlines claim they do not overbook because Japanese travelers wouldn't dream of missing a flight they had reserved a seat on. 🖫

ABANDONED NEW YORK SUBWAY STATIONS #4

18 STREET

LOCATION: AT 18 STREET AND PARK AVENUE
OPENED IN OCTOBER 1904, CLOSED NOVEMBER 1948.

Much like Worth Street, the station is just below street level and has no mezzanine. Unlike Worth Street, however, after a first platform extension in 1910, the post-WWII platform extensions that occurred across the city brought about the closure of 18 St. Since it had only been opened as a half-mile stop between stations, the transit authority deemed it surplus to requirements. There are two short platforms and an unremarkable station. It was so ordinary when built that it was used for publicity photographs for the subway as an example of how all stations looked. ᴥ

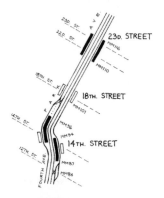

THE SECRET RESTING PLACE OF THE CROSS

The Chiesa di Santa Croce in Gerusalemme church in Rome was founded in A.D. 320 by Helena, the mother of the Emperor Constantine the Great. She had traveled to Jerusalem and brought back a collection of Christian relics from the Holy Land. They are now kept in a reliquary dating from the Fascist era, and include fragments of the "true" Cross, thorns from Christ's crown, and the finger that a skeptical St. Thomas used to probe Christ's wounds. ✑

THE SECRET TO UNLOCKING A WOMAN'S SEX DRIVE

There is a scientifically proven way to increase a woman's sex drive, although unfortunately it requires male stamina and the ability to follow through on the common promise to "phone the next day." Which is apparently impossible for most men. The key to unlocking a woman's sex drive is all down to oxytocin, a bonding chemical found in the brain. Oxytocin is known as the human attachment hormone, and its various functions include aiding milk production during lactation and uterine contractions during childbirth. But it's the fact that the hormone is also released by both sexes during orgasm that holds the key to the female sex drive. Women naturally have oxytocin in spades, and their levels shoot up even more during sexual intercourse. Oxytocin in turn stimulates testosterone production, the hormone responsible for the sex drive in both men and women, which is why the more a woman has sex, the more she will want it.

A man's oxytocin levels, on the other hand, can be up to ten times lower than the average woman's, even a woman who is celibate. In fact, the only time a man's levels reach a point anywhere near a woman's is when he ejaculates. But his oxytocin levels will quickly fall again post-sex. Which is why he won't phone the next day, even if he said he loved you and could never live without you. Sorry, but that was just his oxytocin speaking. ✳

FRYING PAN SECRETS

In terms of non-stickability and even control of heat, cast iron is the best material for a frying pan, closely followed by heavy-weight aluminum. Stainless steel is the worst.

Non-stick frying pans have a much shorter life than you might expect: When even slightly worn, overheating can cause the surface to release potential carcinogens, noxious gases, and tiny particles that can get into the lungs.

Professional chefs will "prove" a new metal pan with oil before its first use. Pour cooking oil into the pan to a depth of about 0.8 inch, heat it up on the stove until very hot but not smoking; pull to the side of the stove—or put it on the lowest heat possible—for at least six hours (overnight is ideal). Dispose of the oil and wipe the pan out with a clean, dry cloth.

Ideally, a metal frying pan should never be washed up. A wipe with a clean, dry cloth should suffice. Any moisture will make food stick. To "prove" a moist pan with salt: Cover its bottom with a thick layer of household salt; heat until the salt starts to turn brown and you can see residual water bubbling out of the metal. Dispose of the salt and wipe the pan out with a clean dry cloth. 🖫

THE MOST EXPENSIVE SECRET IN ROCK & ROLL

Cost TV executive Dick Ebersol $50,000 in August 2003. That's the donation he paid to a charity nominated by Carly Simon on condition she reveal to him the true identity of the man who inspired her 1972 hit, "You're So Vain." Ever since its release, speculation has run rife about the song's subject. Is it Warren Beatty? Kris Kristofferson? James Taylor? They were all at one time or another paramours to Ms. Simon, after all. For years, the rumor mill had a certain rock knight as the subject—and, coincidentally, one of the song's backing singers was Mick Jagger. But Carly had always kept schtum, until she revealed the subject to the curious Mr. Ebersol (who was under strict instructions to keep it to himself). ◠

NIXON'S SECRET *APOLLO 11* SPEECH

President Richard Nixon was prepared in the event of the *Apollo 11* mission ending in catastrophe. His speechwriter William Safire drew up a text for the president to deliver in case Neil Armstrong and Edwin "Buzz" Aldrin were left stranded on the moon. "Fate has ordained that the men who went to the moon to explore in peace will stay on the moon to rest in peace. These brave men, Neil Armstrong and Edwin Aldrin, know that there is no hope for their recovery. But they also know that there is hope for mankind in their sacrifice . . ." To a shocked and grieving world, Nixon would have invoked the spirit of wonder and discovery represented by the astronauts: "In ancient days, men looked at stars and saw their heroes in the constellations. In modern times, we do much the same, but our heroes are epic men of flesh and blood . . ." The final words of the speech echoed the verse of

Rupert Brooke, the English war poet. This time, however, the theme was not patriotism, but pride in humanity itself: "For every human being who looks up at the moon in the nights to come will know that there is some corner of another world that is forever mankind." Fortunately, the speech was never delivered and on 20 July 1969, Armstrong and Aldrin became the first men to walk on the moon. ✍

THE SECRET OF THE TEMPLE SLOT MACHINE

The slot machine is supposed to have been invented in San Francisco in the 1890s by Charles Fey, who designed the Liberty Bell, a heavy, cast-iron machine. His slot machine was a gambling toy and clearly related to the metal boxes that line the casino aisles of Vegas today. However, slot machines—used for revenue-gathering rather than gambling purposes—were known as early as the first century A.D. The engineer and automata-maker Heron of Alexandria constructed the earliest-known example of a slot machine, which was used in temples. Before entering to worship, everyone had to wash their face, and hands. After putting a heavy, probably bronze, coin in the slot of Heron's machine, enough water would come out of the small tap on the front of it for a ritual hand and face wash. The gadget was based on a lever and valve system: The weight of the coin pushed down one end of a lever, and the other end lifted a valve that allowed water to flow out. As the lever was lowered, the coin fell off, and the mechanism returned to its balanced position, shutting off the supply of water. The money in this ingenious invention would be regularly collected by the priests. ᕦ

THE MANY SECRETS OF EGGS

Fresh eggs will have a rough, chalky texture to the outside of the shell; the older the eggs are the smoother the shell will feel.

To determine the freshness of an egg, place it into a glass of water. If it lies down horizontally it is only a day or two old; if it sits at a 45-degree angle it is between a week and 10 days old, and if it stands up vertically it is considerably older than that.

If you shake an egg and you can feel defined movement inside, then it is old. Because the moisture content of eggs diminishes over time, the contents shrink and the air pocket at the rounded ends expands.

When cracked and put in a pan, a fresh egg's yolk will stand up almost spherically and the proportion of thick white to thin white will be much greater. The older it is the more it will spread across the pan's surface.

If you are separating egg yolks and whites, use fresh eggs, because the membrane surrounding the yolk disintegrates with age and is far more likely to spill yolk into the white. If eggs are old, chill them before separating as the lower temperature will toughen the yolk's membrane.

Slightly older eggs are better for hard boiling—it is often difficult to remove shells from very fresh hard-boiled eggs.

Once you have taken hard-boiled eggs off the stove, place the saucepan under a running tap until the water is cold. This stops the eggs cooking in their own heat and prevents a grayish green ring from appearing around the yolks.

Very fresh eggs take longer to boil, so add 30 seconds to the time you would usually cook them for.

For total accuracy, many chefs use eggs by weight in recipes. As a rule of thumb, the contents of a large egg weigh around 1.6 ounces and a medium egg about 1 ounce. About two-thirds of an egg's weight is white, the remaining third is yolk.

Eggshells are porous. Storing eggs near anything with a strong aroma can taint their taste. Leave them in their cartons, the papier-mâché will absorb anything.

Eggs will keep for several weeks in a cool room and be less susceptible to corrupting odors than in the fridge.

When cooked, the whites of eggs straight from the fridge will toughen far more than they would if they had been at room temperature. Remove them from the fridge an hour before cooking.

When boiled, eggs straight from the fridge are likely to crack on contact with water. Use a small pan, leaving less scope for bumping about and cracking. A spoonful of vinegar in the water helps protect shells and stops the white leaking out if it does crack.

When thickening a hot liquid with eggs or egg yolks, add the liquid to the eggs in a bowl away from the stove to avoid separation or curdling. If you do have to add eggs to something being heated, do not stir raw eggs into boiling liquid as the egg will cook and harden before you can whisk it in. Let it cool slightly (to below 150 degrees F, as that's the temperature at which eggs coagulate) first.

If you have leftover egg whites, it's fine to freeze them.

A pinch of cream of tartar, added before you start whisking, will give egg white an extra lift and greater frothiness.

Egg whites have to be free from any corrupting substances if they are to be beaten to stiffness. Whisks and bowls should be clean and grease free, and any specks of yolk should be removed— either scooped out with the egg's shell or dabbed up with a dampened, clean cloth.

Never beat egg whites in an aluminum bowl; it will turn them gray.

Do not cook, fry, or scramble eggs on a very high heat, as fast cooking causes egg whites to toughen.

For perfect scrambled eggs, always undercook them. It doesn't matter that they look far too runny in the pan—they will continue cooking in their own heat as you serve them.

If scrambling eggs in a microwave, when you remove them and beat them during the process, always allow the bowl to stand for 30 seconds or so before continuing to cook. This will let the eggs cook in their own heat before you return them to the microwave and means you can more accurately judge the minimum time required for cooking, thus producing the fluffiest scrambled eggs. 🖫

THE SECRET OF ETERNAL YOUTH

"THE SECRET OF STAYING YOUNG IS TO LIVE HONESTLY,
EAT SLOWLY, AND LIE ABOUT YOUR AGE."
Lucille Ball (*20th-century American comedienne*)

THE DESERT PLANT'S SECRET OF SURVIVAL

We expect a desert by definition to be a barren place. Apart from the odd oasis, which may sport a tall coconut tree or (in American deserts, certainly) a cactus or two, one does not expect to see much vegetation. But it is there, hidden from view.

In the deserts of South Africa, where not much grows, any plant that dares to show its face is asking for trouble. In such a barren environment, if you are alive and green you will get eaten. So, if you are a plant at the bottom of the food chain like the Living Stone, you need a good disguise. Luckily, it has just that.

Short and very squat in a kind of browny-beige color, it looks just like a rock or a stone. Which, of course, is the perfect camouflage when you live in a desert full of stones. Problem solved. ✍

LONG ISLAND SOUND'S SECRET DEAD

Hart Island, off the shore of the Bronx in Long Island Sound, is where the city buries its unclaimed dead. During the Civil War the island was used to house Confederate prisoners, but since the late 1860s it has been the final resting place for New York's indigent and unknown. The cemetery is supervised by the Department of Corrections and prisoners from Riker's Island are ferried in each day from nearby City Island to work there. In the Second World War, Hart Island once again held prisoners of war, including the crew of a German U-boat captured nearby. In the mid-1950s a Nike surface-to-air missile battery was established on the island as a defense against Soviet attack. Although the base was closed in 1961, rendered obsolete by advances in military technology, many of the rusting facilities are still in place. The island is closed to the public. ✍

SECRETS OF VIRAL MARKETING

A popular method of so-called "viral marketing" involves exploiting the relative anonymity of the Internet. Willing collaborators, some of them teenagers, are given free merchandise in return for flooding chat rooms and message boards with multiple rave reviews and detailed accounts of new films.

At the more creative end of the scale, those often subversive reworkings of current film posters that get sent around via e-mail may well have started life in the marketing department of the film's studio. ⌛

THE SECRET OF BARGAIN HUNTING (FOOD)

Do end-of-day shopping. At closing time, many bakeries sell their produce at knocked-down prices. Fruit and vegetable sellers often do the same.

Don't shop with your children. Shopping with children adds around 30 percent to your normal grocery bill.

Don't shop on an empty stomach. As tempting as this sounds, it is never a good idea—you will spend on average between 17 and 20 percent more on your food groceries.

Be focused. In a supermarket, staple items are purposefully placed at the four corners of the store, meaning shoppers are more likely to go off-list. So don't be put off your predetermined course of shopping. ❀

THE SECRET OF THOSE FOOTPRINTS AT GRAUMAN'S CHINESE THEATER

This landmark restaurant in Los Angeles is renowned for the foot- and handprints made in the cement outside by the movie greats of Hollywood. Yet it wasn't a great feat of marketing that brought about the pavement full of prints.

It was an accident. The first stars officially to leave their mark were Mary Pickford and Douglas Fairbanks. But in fact actress Norma Talmadge established the tradition in 1927—when she stumbled into wet cement outside the newly built theater by accident. ৶

THE SECRET LIFE OF THE BOND THEME

The best-known film theme of all time has to be Monty
Norman's "James Bond Theme." But it wasn't written for
Bond. It began life as a tune called "Bad Sign, Good Sign,"
which Norman had written as a sitar instrumental for an
unproduced stage production of V. S. Naipaul's *A House For
Mr. Biswas*. △

CHURCHILL'S SECRET BUNKER

During the wartime bombing of London, British Prime Minister
Winston Churchill governed from underground Cabinet War Rooms
in Whitehall. However, an alternative secret bunker, codenamed
Paddock, was constructed in Dollis Hill in northwest London. This
two-story bunker under Brook Road was completely bombproof
and designed to accommodate 200 cabinet and staff members. It
was to have been used as a last resort in the event of a German
invasion. Churchill stayed there once but apparently didn't find
it to his taste.

A trip to Dollis Hill today will reveal how the ground-level site above has been developed into houses, but there are still two secret entrances to the listed bunker: one via a discreet steel door in a wall between two houses, and the other through a one-story brick building.

In central London, there were several other, smaller fortified bunkers built in the 1930s. These are to be found under Curzon Street in Mayfair, at Montague House in Whitehall, at Storey's Gate, in Horseferry Road, and on Horseguards Parade. None of which ever hosted an evening with Winston Churchill. ⌒

THE SECRET OF LIFE

"THE SECRET OF LIFE IS HONESTY AND FAIR DEALING. IF YOU CAN FAKE THAT, YOU'VE GOT IT MADE."
Groucho Marx (*20th-century American comedian*)

"PART OF THE SECRET OF A SUCCESS IN LIFE IS TO EAT WHAT YOU LIKE AND LET THE FOOD FIGHT IT OUT INSIDE."
Mark Twain (*19th-century American author*)

THE SECRETS OF SUCCESSFUL PERSUASION

Marketing gurus know there are a number of psychologically based marketing tricks guaranteed to make consumers buy things they don't need. But why leave these secrets to the boardroom? Translate the following golden rules of persuasion into every part of your life, and watch your influence soar.

CREATE AN ILLUSION OF SCARCITY

This encourages a sense of urgency, prompting people to act more quickly—and therefore more impulsively—than they usually would. It also creates an impression of exclusivity since the snob-factor adds instant value.

APPRECIATE THE POWER OF RECIPROCITY

The theory here is that when someone gives you something of perceived value, you immediately want to give something back, however subconscious that feeling may be. For instance, a shampoo sample free with a magazine will incite a customer to pick that new shampoo when next faced with a pharmacist shelf.

DEMONSTRATE AUTHORITY

People want the best and the ultimate, so create the impression that what you are pushing is just that. This authority can be an illusion. Studies show stores that play classical music find it easier to sell more expensive items than ones playing pop music; customers automatically feel more refined. Consider commitment and consistency. Stability and reliability may not be the sexiest of qualities, but since both generate trust, they are ultimately invaluable. ❀

ABANDONED NEW YORK SUBWAY STATIONS #5

MYRTLE AVENUE AND DE KALB AVENUE

LOCATION: AT MYRTLE AVE., DE KALB AVE., AND FLATBUSH AVE.

OPENED IN JUNE 1915, CLOSED JULY 1956.

A part of the same Manhattan Bridge Dual System (originally called the Brooklyn Loop Line) as De Kalb Avenue Station (opened June 1915, closed 1960). Myrtle Avenue was a local stop in the

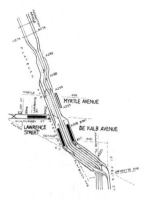

middle of the expressway and originally planned (in 1908) to have five tracks. De Kalb was to have six. However, as the subway system was redrawn and developed, things changed. Eventually four tracks would run through Myrtle Avenue and despite a plan for the Myrtle Ave. El to be above the subway station, after Flatbush Avenue was extended over it in 1909 those plans were dropped. Many people consider the failure to build the elevated station there one of the major missed opportunities of the New York transit system. De Kalb proved to be a serious choke point for the subway system and in 1956 a major rebuild of the area began. Myrtle was bypassed, its southbound platform removed, and the northbound left but abandoned. By 1960 many of the De Kalb platforms had also become obsolete. Since 1980 Myrtle Avenue has been home to a piece of installation art by Bill Brand. Originally designed to be an animated cartoon, it has long since ceased to move and is almost obliterated by dirt and graffiti. ✐

SECRETS OF UNDERCOVER MARKETING

In the 1950s, when television became a mass-market medium, the idea of advertisements was considered new, of course, but it was also considered something of a service to the public. Ads were designed to offer labor-saving devices to the hard-working mothers of America, and they were filmed to look as much like a mini movie as possible. Salesmen and women were friendly types with open faces and winning smiles. The message that they were selling was clear and obvious. Forty years later, however, the public was showing distinct signs of advertising fatigue. Obvious "sells" were derided as cheap and exploitative. The public stopped buying into ads. Something had to be done, and so it was. A generation of smart young people in the early 1990s started developing new and subtle ways to sell us things that we didn't need or want in none-too-obvious ways. In the 21st century, advertisers are finding ever more ingenious ways of relieving us of our money. A relatively recent method is "undercover" or "stealth" marketing, whereby the consumer is targeted without knowing it. Such targeting often occurs where the consumer's guard is down, in a bar, perhaps, or a coffee shop. Attractive young people are hired to appear absorbed with a particular product, or to offer to buy their neighbor a cool new drink they have discovered. The curiosity of those around them is provoked and before long the consumer thinks the drink is pretty cool too, and they are asking the company's representative for information—information the planted people are only too willing to provide.

This is a controversial way of going about your business, of course, but companies who have employed such techniques claim that those polled did not have a problem with being sold to in this way. 🜚

WE CAN SEE YOU, MR. BOND

One would assume that the headquarters of Britain's secret services would be, somehow, secret. Yet since 1995 the Headquarters of MI5, the British Security Service, have been openly located at Thames House, 11 Millbank. Previously, it had been based on Curzon Street, and before that at 140 Gower Street, nicknamed "Russia House."

Farther upstream, on the other side of the river, is Vauxhall Cross, the new headquarters of MI6, the Secret Intelligence Service. It was "blown up" in the opening scenes of the 1999 James Bond film *The World Is Not Enough*. The movie and, therefore, MI6 headquarters were shown widely around the world, making them a very badly kept secret. ✍

THE SECRET OF REMEMBERING NAMES

Picture the scene. You're at a party talking to an acquaintance, wracking your brain trying to remember their name, all the while delaying introducing them to anyone else in case you're found out. What's the one thing worse than someone forgetting your name? Suffering the embarrassment of forgetting someone else's. So here are some secret methods to ensure you will never, ever find yourself in that toe-curling situation again.

PAY CAREFUL ATTENTION TO THE NAME WHEN YOU ARE INTRODUCED TO SOMEONE

Say his or her name to yourself again. Then try and bring it into the ensuing conversation as much as possible to reinforce your memory. This will also ensure you are pronouncing their name correctly.

DON'T BE AFRAID TO ASK HOW TO SPELL A DIFFICULT NAME

If you know the spelling, you can picture this in your mind and you should remember it better. Once alone, write down the new name several times, all the while picturing the person's face.

PAINT A PICTURE

Visual images are powerful memory tools. If you meet someone called Rachel Moss, for instance, imagine her sitting on a mossy knoll.

TRY MAKING UP A RHYME

Rhyming is an excellent way to boost the memory—why else do you think they are so effective for teaching children? If you meet a Jane who looks plain, you won't forget.

LINK A NAME WITH A PERSON'S PROFESSION

"Phil does ills," for instance, might help you recall the name of a medical doctor.

THINK OF A WORD ASSOCIATION

If you meet a Mr. Auld, who is old, hold that thought.

And finally, if all the above fails and you draw a blank, lure someone else—whose name you remember—into the conversation. Say, perhaps, "I'd like you to meet my friend X." The other person should then introduce him- or herself. ⚘

GLENN MILLER: SECRET WEAPON

On 30 October 1944, Glenn Miller and his U.S. Air Force band recorded a special session at the Abbey Road studios in London. These recordings were made for the American Broadcast Station in Europe and the intended audience was the German military; in other words, Glenn Miller's tunes were to be a subtle secret weapon in the wars for hearts and minds. The band was referred to as "A true symbol of America, where everybody has the same rights. It is equal regardless of race, color, and religion." The session was introduced in German by the bandleader himself, helped by translator Ilse Weinberger. Some of the band's standards were sung in German by vocalist Johnny Desmond. The band recorded enough music that day for six programs, which were cheekily transmitted over the airwaves as "Music for the Wehrmach." ✐

THE SPIDER CRAB'S SURVIVAL SECRET

The spider crab's disguise is perfect. It makes use of the hook-like hairs covering its shell and legs to attach algae and other detritus

from the seabed to its body, including the odd sea anemone. With its living camouflage jacket, whether on the move or lying doggo in the sand or silt, the spider crab is indistinguishable from the seabed. ᧒

SECRET LOTIONS AND POTIONS

Wheatgrass may be something of a magic potion when it comes to detoxing and cleansing the system, and, apparently, reducing the effects of aging. But unless it is consumed within 15 minutes of juicing it won't have any effect as the high chlorophyll content evaporates.

Don't wash your daily vitamin supplements down with your morning cup of tea or coffee, as it will block many of the vitamins and minerals being absorbed into your system. Likewise, large amounts of tea and coffee can affect a person's overall levels of nutrient intake.

Creatine is marketed as something of a miracle healer and memory booster, but heavy use can play havoc with our digestion—which is why professional athletes have named it "Creatine havoc."

Prolonged exposure to fluorescent lighting can set off a chemical reaction that will drastically deplete many fruits' and vegetables' nutrient levels.

Much is made of green tea's and red wine's antioxidant content (antioxidants inhibit cell deterioration that can lead to cancer and the visible effects of aging), but by far the best source is cocoa powder. Serving for serving, top-quality cocoa powder will have around three times the antioxidant properties of green tea and even more than that of red wine.

In China, shiitake mushrooms are seen as the secret to a long life; in the western world research has shown them to lower LDL (bad) cholesterol levels and even be effective in halting advanced cancers.

Turmeric is very good in combatting the sort of scalp problems that may lead to hair loss.

A GENIUS'S SECRET

"THE SECRET OF GENIUS IS TO CARRY THE SPIRIT OF THE CHILD INTO OLD AGE, WHICH MEANS NEVER LOSING YOUR ENTHUSIASM."
Aldous Huxley (*20th-century British author*)

THE SECRET HISTORY OF FIREWORKS

The ancient Chinese used fireworks at celebrations such as New Year, weddings, or the birth of children because they believed the loud bangs would scare off evil spirits and ensure good fortune. The sole purpose of these early fireworks was to make as much noise as possible, and it was later that other chemicals were added to produce different colored explosions.

※　※　※

Handel's explosive "Music For The Royal Fireworks" was commissioned by King George I in 1716 to celebrate the signing of a peace treaty with Austria.

※　※　※

In fireworks manufacture, the basic chemical powders added to the gunpowder to create different colored explosions are (subtler shades are created by blending them):

Red	Strontium nitrate	Green	Chlorate or
Orange	Iron		barium nitrate

Yellow	.... Sodium	White	.... Magnesium or
Blue	.... Copper		aluminum. 🖫

THE SECRET BOND BOY

The 1981 James Bond movie *For Your Eyes Only* was in many ways the usual mix of cars, girls, gloriously implausible plotlines, and gadgets, but this movie had a difference: One of the actresses proud to call herself "girl at pool" had once upon a time been a guy. Caroline Cossey's sex-change operation had taken place in 1974, although she had changed her name to Caroline in 1972. Several years after the operation she embarked on a successful modeling career and was cast in the Bond movie in 1980.

After two failed attempts at marriage—one was not allowed because she was still male in the eyes of English law, the other was annulled after her husband left her not long after the honeymoon—she wrote two books and resumed her modeling career. She is now married to a Canadian named David Finch. ⏳

THE SECRET OF *CASABLANCA*'S ALTERNATE ENDING

One of the most popular movies of all time, *Casablanca* began life when playwright Murray Burnett visited the cabaret "La Belle Aurure" in Cap Ferrat during the summer of 1938. He fashioned a play that he called *Everybody Comes to Rick's*. The studio that would make the movie of the play, Warner Bros., changed the title.

There has been a wealth of rumors attached to the film over the years. For instance, despite persistent rumors to the contrary, Ronald Reagan was never the original choice for the role of Rick, although he was considered for the role of Victor Laszlo. George Raft *was* suggested for Rick, but eventually the role went to Humphrey Bogart, of course, who at that time was hot off *The Maltese Falcon*. Ann Sheridan (*Angels with Dirty Faces*; *The Man Who Came to Dinner*) and Hedy Lamarr (*Algiers*; *White Cargo*) were both considered for the role of Ilsa before it went to Ingrid Bergman.

There have long been stories of an alternate ending to the film and there almost was one. In light of the Allied landings at Casablanca, which took place just prior to the film's opening, studio bosses argued for a final scene showing Bogart and Claude Rains on board a ship, listening to a patriotic speech by President Roosevelt. Fortunately, producer Hal Wallis insisted on the now classic shot of Bogart remarking to Rains, as they stroll off into the fog: "Louis, I think this is the beginning of a beautiful friendship." ♤

FUNERAL PARLOR SECRETS

1 Shopping around for funeral services can save you thousands of dollars.

2 Funeral homes are businesses; funeral directors are businessmen, not clergy.

3 Seeing your loved one's body prior to embalming will not increase your grief, and public viewings without embalming are only illegal in Minnesota.

4 Embalming is usually unnecessary if burial is to take place between 24 and 48 hours after death; refrigeration is an alternative that some experts even say is preferable.

5   Sealed caskets do not preserve a body.
6   There is no need to spend more than $400–$600 on a
     casket.

Note: While we're on the subject: There is no hard evidence to
      suggest that the preservatives in food are slowing the de-
      composition of corpses. ⧖

THE SECRET TO GETTING AN UPGRADE

Although a certain degree of luck is involved in getting an upgrade on commercial air flights—they only happen if economy
is full—there are still ways of vastly improving your chances of
having more legroom and better food.

First, consider signing up for an airline loyalty card. If you have
managed to accrue sufficient air miles, the staff might upgrade
you for free. Also, while standing in the check-in line, watch the
staff and adopt your approach accordingly. If the staff member
has been on the receiving end of a screaming match from an
angry passenger, be super-sympathetic when it's your turn. Alternatively, become the person who complains—but do it nicely.

If you have a genuine grievance, air your view and then ask, politely, about the possibility of an upgrade. And never give up. Keep asking at different locations—the check-in, the lounge, or the gate. Nothing is ever set in stone until you enter the plane. Still, certain features are surefire winners if you hope to turn left for free when you step on that plane. Research has proved that people with double-barreled surnames are far more likely to receive upgrades, as indeed are well-spoken men aged between 45 and 55. ✿

THE SECRET TO EATING RIGHT #1

Green tea protects your teeth and can help stop bad breath, as it kills bacteria found in the mouth and the flavoids contained within the leaves work with the active ingredients in toothpaste and mouthwash to boost their efficiency.

A strong cup of coffee before a workout can raise your heart rate and allow you to warm up quicker.

A high-protein meal can increase your memory powers. Immediately. A protein burst will raise your levels of amino acids, which boost your short-term memory for up to three hours.

A couple of drinks a day can help you stay sharp. Pan-European studies showed that those with a drinking-in-moderation culture such as France and Italy had better memories and sharper reactions, as small amounts of alcohol lowered LDL cholesterol, raising blood flow with no added strain in the heart, and therefore carrying more oxygen to the brain.

A WHISPERING GALLERY IN NEW YORK

St. Paul's Cathedral in London has a famous Whispering Gallery and New York has its own version at Grand Central Station. It is on the dining concourse, near the Oyster Bar, and takes the form of a vaulted tiled dome resting on four piers. The acoustics operate in such a way that a whisper from someone standing at one corner can be heard clearly by a listener standing diagonally across.

THE SECRET OF CREATIVITY

"THE SECRET TO CREATIVITY IS KNOWING HOW TO HIDE
YOUR SOURCES."
Albert Einstein (*20th-century German physicist*)

"CREATIVITY COMES FROM TRUST. TRUST YOUR INSTINCTS.
AND NEVER HOPE MORE THAN YOU WORK."
Rita Mae Brown (*20th-century American author*)

THE SECRETS OF IMPRESSING WOMEN

Neuro-linguistic programming (NLP) is a psychological tool discovered in the 1970s that uses language to communicate with the unconscious mind. It is the art of verbal persuasion, a kind of everyday hypnosis that can subtly alter a person's perception. NLP-related tricks have proved extremely successful in dating, since the right kind of language can mean the two of you feel instantly connected. According to the principles of NLP, you should ask your lady friend a question and then match the language of her answer for the rest of the night. For example, ask her, "What do you find most fulfilling about your job?" This should elicit a response that includes such suggestive double-entendres as "passionate" and "stimulating."

Take note of the words she uses most frequently and keep repeating these favorite words of hers. She will feel an instant attraction—and have no idea why.

Or ask her to talk about a happy event from her past. While relaying this joyous anecdote she will subconsciously be transferring these fond memories onto you. Again, she will automatically feel connected to you.

A slightly more sinister NLP concept is using innocent phrases that sound like something else. "It's not below me to do that," for instance, could subconsciously be translated as "Blow me." Alternatively, bring into the conversation the subject of attractive men, maybe how you admire George Clooney for being the kind of man women adore and other men admire. While stating your opinions— beginning with "I think . . ." and so forth—emphatically pat your chest: The woman will instantly relate this talk of gorgeous George to you. ✿

THE SECRET OF SUCCESSFUL PUBLIC SPEAKING

Speaking in public is one of the greatest fears of modern life. It doesn't come easily to most people, including politicians, which is why they employ crack squads of speech writers. Since most of us do not have the means to employ speech writers, we need to know the secrets of how to do it:

Relax. In order to avoid speaking with a squeaky voice, you will need to relax your body before you start. Shrug your shoulders, roll your neck, and make sure you are standing with an equal balance on both feet. Take a deep breath and then begin.

Keep it short. And, where appropriate, entertaining. Light-heartedness and brevity will ensure that the audience stays on your side.

Don't overprepare. And never write your speech out verbatim—reading from a script will make your speech sound dull. Instead, stick to two or three bullet points. Know your subject thoroughly and work around these points.

Consider your audience. Tailor your speech, jokes, and so forth to whomever you are addressing.

Make eye contact. Look at different people in the crowd, and don't focus on a single fixed point. If it makes you feel uncomfortable, look above your audience's heads rather than directly at their faces.

Speak slowly and clearly.

Change your tone. Emphasize key words—that way, any important points you have made will hopefully stick in the mind of your audience.

Consider adding a dramatic pause. This trick will alert the audience—and wake them up. So pause—and then punch.

Include your emotions. Scattering your speech with phrases such as "I feel" will endear you to your audience and make you appear more human.

Think in threes. The great Roman orator Cicero invented this device—the tripartite sentence—as a way of emphasizing his point. If you are including examples, for instance, always include them in threes, saving the most important one for last.

Control your hands. Don't hold them behind your back (it gives the impression that you're hiding something and distracts the audience) or clasp them in front, which can look too much like you are praying. Relax them by holding a pen in your free hand to avoid any awkwardness.

Control your feet. If you are moving around or rocking from side to side, the audience will be distracted from what you are saying. Instead, imagine your feet are set in concrete and you won't move an inch. ❀

SECRET U.S. BIOLOGICAL WARFARE EXPERIMENTS

During the Cold War the U.S. military conducted secret germ warfare experiments on unwitting human subjects. In 1951, army scientists released supposedly harmless microorganisms at the Norfolk Naval Supply Center in Virginia. Similar experiments on how bacteria might spread among the wider population were carried out at Washington National Airport in 1965. The traveling public were exposed to biological agents in a secret simulation of a germ warfare attack. In the 1970s it was revealed that bacteria and a variety of chemicals had been sprayed over the cities of St. Louis, San Francisco, and over another 200 populated areas since the 1950s. The army strongly denied that any of the microorganisms could cause any harm, although mysterious illnesses and deaths have been linked to the experiments. On occasions, deadly substances have been used. In Utah in 1968, around 6,000 sheep were killed after the army released nerve gas 20 miles away. ✎

THE SECRET HISTORY OF IVORY SOAP

Procter & Gamble's Ivory Soap is said to have been so-named after Mr. Proctor had an epiph-any when he heard the following quotation from Psalms in church: "All thy garments smell of myrrh and aloes and cassia, out of the ivory palaces whereby they have made thee glad." Which might be true and makes a good story anyway. The soap's most remarkable property, though, is that it floats. According to Proctor & Gamble folklore, this neat marketing trick came about by accident in the mid- to late-nineteenth century.

The story goes that in 1879, a hapless young employee who had been instructed to switch the soap mixing machine off at lunchtime forgot to do so, which resulted in more air being added to the soap than was normal, giving it a softer, fluffier texture. Hapless new boy told his supervisor about the blunder, goes the story, and they agreed to continue the production process as normal, packaging the soap and sending it out, hoping that no one would notice.

But before long, Proctor & Gamble were receiving letters saying how the soap was suddenly revolutionizing people's lives. Women were saying that the whole process of washing had been changed because the soap floated. The bosses sought the source of the change in its constituency and found hapless new boy and his accidental new technique. Both were retained, giving the soap its defining feature.

But there is recent evidence to suggest that this lovely story is just that—a story. Researchers hunting through company archives while in the process of compiling a book about the company found the diary of James N. Gamble, son of the Proctor & Gamble's co-founder. One 1863 entry reads: "I made floating soap today. I think we'll make all of our stock that way." ⧗

FLIGHT CONTROL SECRETS #1

Just as French is the language of the professional kitchen, English is the language of the skies: Everywhere in the world pilots and air traffic controllers communicate in English.

※ ※ ※

On flights, the pilots will be served the same meals as first-class passengers, but they are not permitted to have the same dish for fear of food poisoning. For this reason they are not allowed to eat identical meals prepared in the same kitchen during the six hours before a flight.

※ ※ ※

It's common practice among cabin crew to take the odd blast of pure oxygen from the emergency cylinders to keep themselves sharp on long-haul or overnight flights.

※ ※ ※

The amount of time cabin crew have off between shifts varies enormously from airline to airline as every country's aviation authority views it differently: American cabin crew have longer maximum shifts (19 hours) than British-based staff (16.5 hours) and a shorter minimum rest period (8 hours) as opposed to a full 24-hour-day's rest if they have worked the maximum length.

※ ※ ※

It costs between $100,000 and $200,000 to train a pilot to commercial airline standards. Training can take up to 14 months, and that will be with previous flying experience—either in the Forces or light aircraft—as a background.
Only 15 percent of all pilot applications received by British Airways are accepted for training.

THE SECRET OF LOVE

> "LOVE CEASES TO BE A PLEASURE WHEN IT
> CEASES TO BE A SECRET."
> Aphra Behn (*17th-century British playwright*)

THE SECRET OF BEING A GOOD BOSS

You may have been taught to perform a multitude of job-related skills to perfection, but few of us are ever taught the secret of how to be a good boss. Here's the secret of how to achieve that.

To really succeed as a boss, you need to become a psychopath. Yes, really. According to recent research by a British university, the vast majority of office managers have personality traits that are almost identical with criminal psychopaths—in other words, psychiatric patients and hospitalized criminals—only altered by the fact they are law-abiding and marginally less impulsive. These traits include: the ability to be emotionally detached, egocentric, a mindless perfectionist, an expert in turning on the superficial charm, and willing to use and discard other people at whim.

Lying, cheating, and general ruthlessness will get you to the top and help to keep you there.

However, if you're not psychopath material, consider the following:

Set a good example for your staff to live up to. Your office moral code should include never taking credit for something another employee has done, being scrupulously honest, and sharing as much company news as feasibly possible with your staff. Do this and you show respect for your workforce, something that will instill company loyalty.

Trust each employee to do their own work to the best of their ability. Define their duties clearly and regularly ask their opinions. Then give continuous feedback and praise good work.

Praise in public; criticize in private.

Really get to know your team—not only their positions but also their home life. If you are starting in a new office, make sure you have a one-on-one meeting with each member of the staff to find out what they hope to achieve and where their ambitions lie.

Fight for what your staff want—if it's a raise, make sure they realize you are doing everything in your power to make it happen.

You should also delegate wisely—you will always achieve more as a team than on your own.

Become a mentor to juniors; show a caring side of your personality that won't be forgotten. In business, what goes around comes around, and today's bright intern could be tomorrow's CEO. ✿

THE TOP 20 SECRETS OF MAKING FRIENDS AND INFLUENCING PEOPLE

How to Win Friends and Influence People was the title of Dale Carnegie's groundbreaking 1937 book, probably the most famous self-help book of all time—it has now sold over 15 million copies. However, the world has changed somewhat since then and so the following advice should prove much more useful in the modern world.

ONE
Make people feel as important and appreciated as they believe they really are.

TWO
Become a good listener. Everyone loves talking about themselves.

THREE
Do not argue. Ever. In an argument, no one ever comes out the winner.

FOUR
If you find yourself the bearer of bad news, think of a way to soften the blow, maybe with a gift.

FIVE
When handling people, never criticize or complain. If you have a criticism to make, start with some praise and appreciation of their performance. Or talk about your own shortcomings before mentioning someone else's.

SIX
Find out—and remember—the names of your boss's kids or their favorite hobbies. He or she will start believing that you fit perfectly into the company, thus making promotion a more likely prospect for you than for a rival colleague who shows no interest.

SEVEN

To make someone do what you want, make them think that it was their idea in the first place.

EIGHT

If you are wrong, admit it instantly and emphatically.

NINE

Make "less is more" your personal mantra. In a business situation, say little and let other people do most of the talking. The same goes for e-mails—if you keep them short there is less scope for misinterpretation.

TEN

Create a mystique about yourself. If you are ever-so-slightly enigmatic and sphinx-like, people are less likely to put you in a box.

ELEVEN

In any situation, try and see it from the other person's point of view.

TWELVE

Ask questions and don't give direct orders.

THIRTEEN

Be encouraging. Praise every improvement.

FOURTEEN
Give people an excellent reputation to live up to.

FIFTEEN
When you are tempted to react to something, ignore your initial feeling and let it go. Knee-jerk reactions do not bode well in business.

SIXTEEN
Make sure that people are dependent on you.

SEVENTEEN
Remember that your reputation is priceless and crucial if you want power. As Warren Buffett, the legendary investor, once said, "It takes 20 years to build a reputation and 5 minutes to ruin it." So never put your name on something you are less than 100 percent proud of.

EIGHTEEN
Work as a team and never become too isolated. Success rarely goes to the outsider; influence never does. You will always need your allies.

NINETEEN
Don't be too perfect. A few well-chosen flaws will make you appear more human. And never perform any task better than your boss—he or she will always want to feel superior and unthreatened.

TWENTY
Remember that it's lonely at the top.

FAMOUS AMERICAN FREEMASONS

BENJAMIN FRANKLIN
U.S. inventor of the lightning rod, 1746

GEORGE WASHINGTON
U.S. president between 1789 and 1797

THEODORE ROOSEVELT
U.S. president between 1901 and 1909

HENRY FORD
U.S. car manufacturer, created the Model T Ford in 1908

J. EDGAR HOOVER
Head of the FBI between 1924 and 1972

CHARLES LINDBERGH
U.S. aviator, made the first solo transatlantic flight, 1927

FRANKLIN D. ROOSEVELT
U.S. president between 1933 and 1945

IRVING BERLIN
U.S. songwriter, author of "White Christmas," 1942

HARLAND SANDER
AKA Col. Sanders, U.S. founder of KFC, created his secret recipe in 1939

HARRY S. TRUMAN
U.S. president between 1945 and 1953

GEORGE C. MARSHALL
U.S. general, chief of staff from 1939 until 1945; winner of Nobel Peace Prize 1953

ROY ROGERS
U.S. actor and professional cowboy, star of his eponymous TV show, 1951–64

DOUGLAS MACARTHUR
U.S. Army general, commander of Allied Forces in the Pacific WWII, 1941–45

ERNEST BORGNINE
U.S. actor, Academy Award–winner in 1955 for best actor in *Marty*

EDWIN "BUZZ" ALDRIN
Astronaut, second man to
walk on the moon, 1969

GERALD FORD
U.S. president between 1974
and 1977. ⌔

THE SECRET OF SUCCESSFUL FLIRTING

Marilyn Monroe, Henry Kissinger, and Bill Clinton were all world-class experts in the art of flirting. Successful flirts aren't necessarily born, however; they can be made, which is why flirting academies are cropping up in many metropolitan cities. Here are some top flirting secrets:

WORK ON YOUR ENTRANCE
INTO A ROOM
Pause when you enter the
room, survey the scene, put
your shoulders back, and then
continue walking.

DON'T BE PART OF A CROWD
It can appear intimidating.
Stand slightly apart from
the rest to signify your
individuality.

MAXIMIZE YOUR DIRECT EYE CONTACT

Hold it for a little longer than is normal, and then immediately lower your eyes.

REPEAT A PERSON'S NAME

This will instantly make them feel special.

CREATE AND USE A NICKNAME

The two of you will form an instant, exclusive bond.

ASK "SOULFUL" QUESTIONS

Such as "Do you believe in love at first sight?" or "Do you love someone because you need them, or need them because you love them?"

MIRROR THE OTHER PERSON'S BODY LANGUAGE

The most revealing body language happens below the waist, so point your feet toward the object of your flirting.

WEAR OR CARRY SOMETHING UNUSUAL

It can be a handy talking point.

BE UPBEAT

Don't dwell on any problems or personal troubles.

REVEAL YOUR INNER WRIST

It makes you appear vulnerable and ripe for seduction.

**AIM FOR AN
ACCIDENTAL TOUCH**
For instance, reach for the door handle at the same time. Sparks will fly.

**SUBTLY RUB YOUR THIGH
IN A RHYTHMICAL AND
REPETITIVE MANNER**
It will subconsciously draw the attention of the person you're talking to toward the groin area. ✿

THE SIMPLE SECRET OF LIVING LONGER

A 15-year Greek study that concluded in the early 21st century contrasted the cardiovascular health and death rates of men and women living in lowland and upland villages, 3,300 feet above sea level. Although their lives were similar in all other respects, the mountain dwellers lived longer and had less heart disease than the plains dwellers. The answer to longer life, researchers concluded, is to move to the mountains. Living in the less oxygen-rich air at moderate altitude causes physiological changes that strengthen heart function. ✎

GONE WITH THE WIND SECRETS

How different it could all have been: Imagine Lucille Ball as Pansy O'Hara in *Baa Baa Black Sheep* . . . or Bette Davis as Angel O'Hara in *Not In Our Stars* . . . or even Mae West as Storm O'Hara in *Tote the Weary Load*. . . . These are just some of the strange ways in which *Gone with the Wind*, the film seen by more people on the planet than any other, could have turned out.

At one time or another, Bette Davis, Lana Turner, Paulette Goddard, Susan Hayward, Katherine Hepburn, and Mae West were all shortlisted for Scarlett O'Hara, the most coveted role in film history. And when the nationwide search came to Atlanta, over 500 Southern belles turned up, including every Miss Atlanta since 1917! In 1939, after three years and more than $4 million spent trying to bring *Gone with the Wind* to the screen, producer David O. Selznick's troubles still weren't over. Author Margaret Mitchell had written Rhett Butler's farewell to Scarlett as "My dear, I don't give a damn." But somewhere along the line "frankly" was added, giving the line greater emphasis and the movie its infamous adieu. In an attempt to minimize offense

and mollify the censors, Clark Gable put the stress on "give" rather than the final swear word. But the censors of the time were not fooled, and fined Selznick $5,000 for including the profanity.

THE SECRETS OF MANIPULATION TECHNIQUES USED BY PRODUCT MANUFACTURERS

We are very obedient when it comes to following instructions on the products we buy, and the manufacturers know it. Famously, back in the 1930s, Lever Brothers asked their employees for suggestions on how to improve their shampoo sales.

One bright spark suggested the addition of the word "Repeat" to the directions written on bottles. Voilà—sales were doubled.

In the 1960s, Alka Seltzer began a marketing campaign to remove its associations with the elderly and with overindulgent slobs who ate and/or drank too much. They did so using humor, but more crucially, although the directions on the packet said it was only necessary to use one tablet, the advertisements featured two tablets clunking and fizzing into a glass of water with a "plop plop, fizz fizz" catchline. The effect on sales was immediately positive.

Consider too the arrival of the tiny words "After opening, refrigerate" and sometimes "Eat within 8 weeks" on sauce bottles. They weren't there when the product was first sold. The benefit to the manufacturer of the latter is obvious: If you obey, you will get through or dispose of the bottle more quickly and replace it with another. The former, however, is brilliant. If you store your bottle in the refrigerator, probably in the door, you will be reminded of it every time you open it. Stuck in a cupboard you will forget it is there and will use it less often. They know us better than we know ourselves. ⌛

THE SECRET SEARCH FOR
THE GOD PARTICLE

There's a secret underground race on to prove the existence of the so-called "God particle" that physicists theorize gives matter its mass, and explains how the universe was made. Nesting 330 feet below the city suburbs of Geneva is a 17-mile tunnel that houses the newly built Large Hadron Collider, the brainchild of particle physicists at Cern, the European-funded Laboratory for Particle Physics.

Near Chicago in the United States is the underground 7-mile Fermilab Tevatron particle accelerator. In these tunnels, high-energy beams of protons and anti-protons will be accelerated around in both directions, so the particles collide. It's hoped the results will show that the God particle or Higg's boson (named after the British physicist Peter Higgs who suggested its existence in the late 1960s) really does exist. ᴕ

THE SECRET TO FINDING A HUSBAND

Adopt the following advice if you want to marry Mr. Right.

MOVE TO THE COUNTRYSIDE

Research proves that statistically there are more single women in cities and, conversely, more single men in rural areas.

GET OUT MORE

Find eligible men in the gym, in coffee shops, or on the train, or join an evening class with a guaranteed high quota of the opposite sex (think military history). Be friendly and make an effort to strike up conversations.

MAKE THE FIRST MOVE

Men are more confused than ever about when it is considered appropriate to pounce. Erase any confusion for him.

DO NOT APPROACH A MAN WHO IS OVER THE AGE OF 40

Again, research shows that the likelihood of a man marrying post-40 (with the exception of divorcés) reduces drastically. These men are confirmed bachelors and set in their unattached ways.

BE SUPER-CONFIDENT ABOUT EVERYTHING FROM THE WAY YOU CARRY YOUR-SELF TO YOUR OPINIONS

Confidence is like catnip.

TAKE CARE OF YOUR APPEARANCE

Make the most of what you have and accentuate the positive. Also, always expose a small amount of flesh—perhaps an ankle, your wrists, or the nape of your neck—as this subconsciously reveals your warm inner nature.

BECOME A GREAT LISTENER

Men love talking about themselves and will feel instantly comfortable in front of a willing audience.

TREAT YOUR SINGLE STATUS AS A BUSINESS PLAN

Announce to everyone you know that you are on the look-out for single men—friends of friends often make the best dates as they have already been vetted. Devote a third of your earnings to self-improvement including expensive haircuts, a new wardrobe, gym membership, etc.

BECOME A PRAYING MANTIS AND DON'T BE AFRAID TO CHASE

Many men eventually submit to highly motivated man-eaters.

You can easily convince a man he can't survive without you— if only because he hasn't been given the chance. ✿

THE SECRET OF BARGAIN HUNTING (ELECTRICAL GOODS)

OFFER TO PAY IN CASH

Even the electrical departments in the most glitzy of department stores may do a deal if you're not using a credit card.

PLAY DUMB

And act friendy. Ask for the salesman's advice. He will be flattered that you are putting your trust in him and will thus be much more likely to offer you a great deal.

ASK FOR EXTRAS

If you feel like haggling, simply ask: "What's the best price you can do this for?" If the salesman is unwilling to offer a discount, ask about free delivery or installation.

GO TO THE LAST DAY OF A TRADE EXHIBITION

Since the exhibitors will be packing up their stands, they might sell their goods off cheap instead of carrying them home. ✿

HOW HARRY HOUDINI DID IT

Harry Houdini was born Ehrich Weiss on 24 March 1874 in Budapest, Hungary. He was undoubtedly the most famous escapologist of all time. To begin with, his feats were relatively simple, involving escaping from handcuffs while in full view of his audience. Later they began to involve immersion in water while being restricted by chains held together by multiple padlocks—this time behind a curtain. It would be wrong to try and uncover all the secret tricks of his trade, but here is a major element of one: When he was chained up, the large padlock he always used could easily be opened and contained keys for all the others. ⌛

THE SECRETS OF REMEMBERING

Age is frequently blamed for a failing memory but advancing years are not always the cause. Like all muscles, the brain needs regular exercise or it will become flabby. So regular mental exercises will help. The next time you find yourself at a loss in the grocery store, consider the following.

MAKE AN EFFORT

If you need to remember something, take notes. Seeing something in writing will get your brain into gear.

CONJURE UP A CLEVER MNEMONIC

After all, we all remember "Never Eat Shredded Wheat" for the points of a compass. It also helps that this particular mnemonic has the added extra of rhyming, which is another excellent memory tool.

USE THE LINK METHOD

This ingenious technique is perfect for remembering lists. The theory is that you link each item on the list to the next by way of a story.

THINK VISUALLY

The majority of people remember things best with a visual picture. Create your own.

HAVE A GOOD NIGHT'S SLEEP

Countless research has proven that if you are not well rested, your memory will be all over the place.

REPEAT YOURSELF

Learning a subject parrot-fashion used to be the preferred teaching method in schools, and for good reason. Repetition ingrains on the brain.

EAT WELL

Supplement your diet with ginkgo biloba, a traditional Chinese medicine extracted from the leaf of the ginkgo plant. And stay away from alcohol—too much booze will make your memory more holey than Swiss cheese.

FLIGHT CONTROL SECRETS #2

Commercial airplanes are so rigorously checked that mechanical or engineering failure now accounts for less than 5 percent of all accidents. Airplanes are checked fully before each flight, and routine checks escalate as flying hours clock up: At 25,000 hours (approximately 5 years) a plane will be stripped right down and rebuilt in a process that takes over a month.

※ ※ ※

Short-haul aircraft are checked far more frequently, as they perform relatively more take-offs and landings, and increase and decrease cabin pressure more frequently, all of which puts a great deal of stress on the aircraft.

※ ※ ※

Dulles International Airport in Washington, D.C., was renamed Washington Dulles Airport during the Reagan years because the president kept getting confused between that and Dallas International in Texas, which was renamed Dallas/Fort Worth.

※　※　※

Don't complain or make too much fuss at check-in. If you read the small print on your ticket very carefully, you will discover that it doesn't entitle you to be flown anywhere—airlines will always have the final word in disputes with passengers as they are not legally obliged to honor your ticket.

※　※　※

Every aircraft in service can be identified by a Hull Number, which is noted on an international register, which keeps a record of service history, repairs, and replaced parts. However, disreputable small airlines are circumventing this procedure through a layer of aircraft traders who buy decommissioned craft for scrap, and sell them back into service without a valid Hull Number. This practice is seen mostly in India and Africa.

※　※　※

Apart from mechanical failure, the most common reason flights (both scheduled and charter) are canceled is because of unsold seats. If an airline hasn't sold enough seats for the flight to at least cover its costs the airline will simply cancel it and distribute the passengers elsewhere. This is particularly noticeable on very early morning scheduled flights.

THE SECRET OF KEEPING A SECRET

"THREE MAY KEEP A SECRET, IF TWO OF THEM ARE DEAD."
Benjamin Franklin (*18th-century American inventor*)

CHEMICAL WARFARE EXPERIMENTS ON THE NEW YORK SUBWAY

In 1966, the U.S. Army carried out biological warfare experiments on the New York Subway without informing the population. A light bulb filled with a harmless bacterium, *Bacillus subtilis variant niger*, was smashed onto the tracks. Within 20 minutes, it had spread throughout the system and affected a million civilians. Experts estimated that had a more deadly organism been released, thousands of lives would have been at risk. ᔕ

THE SECRET OF THE WINCHESTER HOUSE

Sarah L. Winchester came into the Winchester Rifle fortune when her husband William died young of tuberculosis in 1881. Their only child, Anna, had died as a baby and, distraught at this second death, Sarah sought help in spiritualism. She was told by a medium that there was a curse on her family and the souls of those killed by her family's gun business would only rest easy if she traveled west and kept building a house for them to live in—if she stopped the building work, she would die. She moved to San Jose, and started work on what came to be called the Winchester Mystery House. This astonishing building was continually changed and extended until her death in 1922, 36 years later. She had carpenters and builders working 24 hours a day and, by the end, there were 160 rooms (including 40 bedrooms), 47 fireplaces, and a number of curious features, such as staircases that lead nowhere and the recurrence of the number 13 in the design. ✐

THE SUPER SIZE SECRET

Between the years 2000 and 2005, portions in popular restaurants and of pre-packaged food grew progressively larger—in restaurants across the board, they were one-third bigger in 2005 than they were 5 years before. Unbelievably, this was a strategy arrived at by the food industries in order to increase profits, as they couldn't charge any more for food without appearing to give better value.

The secret of how they managed to make it look as if the customer was getting more for their money, while taking more money from the customer is this: The cheaper ingredients and foods—specifically the carbohydrates—were increased out of proportion to the dish itself, meaning a burger or pizza that seemed, for instance, 30 percent bigger only had its manufacturing costs increased by around 10 percent. It also means that the caloric values shot up: Between 2000 and 2005, the caloric content of the average portion of large fries—taken across several well-known fast food outlets—more than doubled from 250 to 600 calories.

This not only vastly hiked the mark-up on processed and mass-produced food, but the perpetual inflating of portion sizes changed the way many people approached buying food, first in restaurants and then in the supermarket. When faced with the apparent value of a jumbo-sized meal, it didn't take long for people to accept these new servings to the point that what used to seem satisfactory suddenly looked positively puny. Restaurant plates got bigger, takeaway cartons subtly increased in size. Then food items got resized on the menu, notably with chocolate bars and pizzas: What was large is now medium and a new size has been added on top. Yet because people are more often than not programed from childhood to finish what's put in front of them, they still eat it all. And still feel hungry after at much the same time as they always have because so much of this new huge meal consists of empty calories, hence they eat another big meal. 🖫

THE COLONEL'S SECRET

Although the actual KFC recipe remains locked in a vault somewhere, probably in deepest Kentucky and guarded by large men in cowboy hats, follow these instructions and your fried chicken will be indistinguishable from the Colonel's finest.

EQUIPMENT:

Two large mixing bowls

A whisk

Large cook's knife and chopping board

A tray for rolling chicken pieces in flour

A deep fat fryer, corn oil, and thermometer

INGREDIENTS:

1 chicken cut into eight pieces for frying

(2–3 breasts, wings, thighs, drumsticks)

2 eggs

½ cup milk

⅔ cup flour (half plain/half self-raising)

4oz fine fresh breadcrumbs (make your own, don't open a packet!)

1 Knorr chicken stock cube

½ teaspoon garlic powder

(not garlic salt, but dried powdered garlic)

½ teaspoon onion powder (not onion salt)

½ teaspoon paprika

1 tablespoon finely chopped fresh parsley

2 large cloves garlic

½ teaspoon salt
½ teaspoon soy sauce
½ teaspoon Worcestershire sauce
2 teaspoons black peppercorns

METHOD:

In one of the mixing bowls, thoroughly beat eggs, milk, soy sauce, and Worcestershire sauce together.

Using the flat of the knife and a corner of the chopping board, grind garlic into a paste with the salt and beat into mixture.

Add half the parsley, the crumbled stock cube, and about a quarter of the flour. Beat in thoroughly to avoid any lumps.

Separate about half the remaining flour onto the tray for rolling the chicken pieces.

In the second mixing bowl, thoroughly combine the other half of the flour and the breadcrumbs.

Crush the peppercorns on the chopping board
under the heel of the knife and add to flour.

Blend in the rest of the ingredients, mixing together
well with your fingers.

Heat oil in deep fat fryer to 360 degrees F. (Oil temperature is
crucial, as too hot oil will burn the coating before the chicken
inside is fully cooked, while too cool will mean the crumbs and
flour absorb the oil to become soggy.)

Roll each piece of chicken in the flour on the tray until thoroughly
coated. (If the flour starts to run out before you have finished coating your chicken, simply top the tray up with extra plain flour.)

Immerse into the egg and milk mixture in the first mixing bowl.

Roll in the flour/breadcrumbs bowl until totally coated.

Lower gently into the hot oil and fry until golden brown in
color—3 or 4 minutes approximately.

Remove from oil and drain on a tray covered in paper towels.

Or—alternative finish—serve in a thin cardboard box that soaks up the surplus oil and subsequently transfers it to your clothes. 🖫

THE REAL BEVERLY HILLBILLIES

The elite Beverly Hills High School at 241 Moreno Drive is the site of a functioning oil derrick. The operation is carefully managed so as to minimize disruption to pupils, but still produces around 600 barrels of oil a day and thousands of dollars a month in revenues for the school and the local community. ✍

AMERICAN PIE SECRETS

Don McLean's "American Pie" reached #1 in in the United States in 1972. At 8 minutes 27 seconds long, it was inspired by the events of 3 February 1959—"the day the music died"—when the plane carrying Buddy Holly, Ritchie Valens, and The Big Bopper crashed into a snowy field, killing everyone on board. McLean's lyrics also referenced Mick Jagger at Altamont ("Satan laughing with delight"), Bob Dylan ("the jester on the sideline in a cast"), and The Beatles ("the quartet practiced in the park").

"American Pie" was written in a single day and the hit version was recorded in just one take. In 1991 Don McLean copyrighted the phrase "American Pie," and he protects it jealously— the makers of the movie *American Pie* had to ask permission to use the title. At the start of the new millennium, this most personal of songs was given a radical makeover when Madonna's cover version reached #1. What does "American Pie" mean to McLean now? "It means," he says, "that I don't have to work if I don't want to." 🔔

THE SECRET HISTORY OF GUNPOWDER

The popular belief that the Chinese discovered gunpowder is vehemently disputed in many circles, notably in the Middle East and the Indian subcontinent, where it is thought that the Moors developed explosives a few hundred years earlier. Apparently, the reason European historians credit the Chinese is because gunpowder arrived in Europe from China courtesy of Marco Polo in the 13th century.

The Moors and the Indians were certainly the first to exploit the weapons potential of gunpowder. The Chinese had the material for several hundred years before they considered making cannons or guns—it had no weapons usage when Marco Polo brought it back. The Moors were recorded using cannon in battle as early as the 12th century. 🖫

THE SECRET OF SUCCESSFUL PARENTING

"PARENTS CAN ONLY ADVISE THEIR CHILDREN OR POINT
THEM IN THE RIGHT DIRECTION. ULTIMATELY PEOPLE SHAPE
THEIR OWN CHARACTERS."
Anne Frank (*20th-century Dutch diarist*)

"THERE ARE TIMES WHEN PARENTHOOD SEEMS NOTHING
BUT FEEDING THE MOUTH THAT BITES YOU."
Peter De Vries (*20th-century American author*)

"CHILDREN AREN'T HAPPY WITHOUT SOMETHING TO IGNORE,
AND THAT'S WHAT PARENTS WERE CREATED FOR."
Ogden Nash (*20th-century American poet*)

"I HAVE FOUND THE BEST WAY TO GIVE ADVICE
TO YOUR CHILDREN IS TO FIND OUT WHAT THEY WANT
AND THEN ADVISE THEM TO DO IT."
Harry S. Truman (*20th-century American president*)

THE SECRETS OF SUCCESSFULLY SELLING YOUR HOUSE

Choose the time of year to sell that best suits your house. If you have a well-stocked, flowering garden for instance, show the house at the height of its flowering. If you have a cozy place that is best shown in the light of a glowing fire, show it in early winter, pre-Christmas. If your swimming pool is a major asset, sell in early summer (but keep people out of the pool while showing).

Try to recall when you bought the house and what attracted you to it—chances are the same things will attract a new buyer. Enhance those features.

First impressions count. Tidy the front yard, give the front door a fresh lick of paint and de-clutter the entrance hall. You may even need to go as far as sweeping public areas like the sidewalk in front of your house—many buyers make their decision on the curb appeal of a property.

Make sure that every room in your house is clean and tidy.

Think about creating a home, not just a house. Buyers want an environment that feels warm. Imagine your potential buyer and market your house accordingly.

Tidy up. It may sound obvious, but unsightly mess doesn't only refer to any unwashed dishes (an obvious no-no) but also to too much clutter. Hide as much as you can from view to create a free-flowing environment.

Get rid of pets. Lots of people don't like them and they can be rather, well, smelly. The same goes for children and their paraphernalia, too.

Bake some bread—yes, this really does work! As does the similarly enticing aroma of freshly brewed coffee. Fresh flowers will also make your house seem more inviting to potential buyers.

Erase anything too "individual" from clear view. Many buyers have firm ideas about how an interior should look and have a difficult time seeing past what, to them, is a mistake. To be absolutely sure that your interior won't upset anyone, it's worth spending a small amount of money on painting your walls in neutral shades.

Bathrooms and kitchens sell houses, so make sure yours are extra-special. Re-tile and re-fit if necessary—the cost of any extra work will be recouped when you sell your home. After all, the last thing you want is a house listed as "needing work."

Market any outside space as an extra room. In other words, add tables, chairs, and seductive lighting.

Lighten up. Put on as many lights and lamps as possible when showing potential buyers around. A dark corner can be a distinct disadvantage when showing a home. Make sure your windows are washed, both inside and out. ✿

SECRETS OF SUVEILLANCE

With the advent of the Internet came a new source of government intelligence-gathering hardware. Possibly the largest and most awe-inspiring invention is ECHELON, a massive computer system that monitors every piece of electronic information that is broadcast or sent over the Internet, anywhere in the world. Stations housing ECHELON hardware are situated around the globe and the information that it gathers is shared between American and British intelligence services.

The surveillance system is programed to identify key words in e-mails and on Web sites, intercept the whole message or content, and file away to be further analyzed by intelligence agents. If there is anyone who might doubt the existence of such a machine or that it could not be used in the West, they should read the following.

It is taken from a July 2001 Report of the European Parliament on the existence of a global system for the interception of private and commercial communications (ECHELON interception system).

(W)hereas the existence of a global system for intercepting communications, operating by means of co-operation proportionate to their capabilities among the USA, the UK, Canada, Australia and New Zealand under the UKUSA Agreement, is no longer in doubt; it seems likely, in view of the evidence and the consistent pattern of statements from a very wide range of individuals and organizations, including American sources, that its name is in fact ECHELON.

Plus, "the interception of communications is a method of spying commonly employed by intelligence services, so that other states might also operate similar systems, provided that they have the required funds and the right locations. France is the only EU Member State which is—thanks to its overseas territories—geographically and technically capable of operating autonomously a global interception system and also possesses the technical and organizational infrastructure to do so. There is also ample evidence that Russia is likely to operate such a system."

So if you were wondering why certain e-mails that you'd sent were not getting to their intended recipient, take a look at the language of your message and remove any possibly "dangerous" words, such as "bomb," "conspiracy," "fatwah," or "Cheney." Resend and then you'll find the message makes it to its destination. But be prepared for a loud knock on your front door at a very early hour of the morning, soon. ᢒᐠ

ROMAN FACE CREAM

In the Tabard Square archaeological ruins in London's Southwark, the remains of the oldest-known cosmetic face cream was excavated in 2003. A small metal canister was found in a drain on the site of a Romano-Celtic temple, and has been dated to the 2nd century A.D. The pot contained a thick white cream with fingermarks inside the lid, presumably those of the Roman lady to whom it belonged. The cream was analyzed and found to contain lead oxide, which whitens the skin, as well as animal fats and starch, to moisturize it. The site is now being developed to provide shops and houses. ᢒᐠ

THE SECRET CHICKEN OF DOWNING STREET

The prime minister of Great Britain lives at number 10 Downing Street in London. The building has been home to the head of the British government since the 18th century, when the last private resident to live there rejoiced in the name of Mr. Chicken (he left in 1735). The street was built at the end of the 17th century by Lord Downing, a former spy for Oliver Cromwell during the English Civil War who switched allegiance after the Roundhead leader died in 1658. What is now number 10 Downing Street was originally number 5. What's less known is that, despite the armed guards and security gates permanently situated at the end of the street, the road is still a public right of way. Politely insist and you will be allowed to walk along Downing Street, albeit with an armed escort. ✍

SECRETS OF WEIGHT LOSS

It takes the brain about 20 minutes to register that the stomach is full, so because we tend to eat more quickly these days, we will overeat—literally—by going past capacity without the brain realizing. Thus a good way to lose weight is simply to eat more slowly.

※ ※ ※

Drastically cutting the calories is far from the most efficient, or even the most successful, way to lose weight. If you reduce your caloric intake to much below what your body needs (and everybody's body has different needs) it will go into "starvation mode" and readjust your metabolism to burn what you are consuming more slowly and still store some as fat for vital functions or emergencies.

※ ※ ※

People who experience the least weight gain in middle age are likely to have a much happier old age. This isn't simply because of the better health aspect, but test studies carried out in Sweden have shown a much higher level of emotional and spiritual well-being too.

※ ※ ※

We ought to eat five small meals a day rather than three, or fewer, huge ones—you wouldn't run your car until the tank was bone dry and then fill it to the point that gas was slopping out over your shoes, would you?

※ ※ ※

Eating yogurt will actually help you lose weight, as the high calcium content provides a catalyst for your body to burn fat more efficiently and will actually limit the amount of fat your body will support.

※ ※ ※

White poultry meat will contain roughly half the intrinsic fat of dark meat. The dark meat (the legs) is made from slow-twitch muscle fibers of the type used for persistent activities such as walking, while the breast is fast-twitch muscle for sudden, occasional movements, and the former requires a greater store of fat to function efficiently.

※ ※ ※

Margarine or vegetable oil spreads have to have less than 65 percent fat to be allowed to call themselves "reduced fat" and 40 percent or less to bear the name "low fat." 💾

LONDON'S CENTERS OF ESPIONAGE

THAMES HOUSE, MILBANK, SW1
Current headquarters of MI5 (Security Service).

EUSTON TOWER, NW1
Center for MI5's "Watcher" surveillance service.

140 GOWER STREET, WC1
MI5 Headquarters 1976–1995.

VAUXHALL CROSS, SE1
Headquarters of MI6 (Secret Intelligence Service).

NEW SCOTLAND YARD, SW1, LONDON
Headquarters of the Special Branch.

THE SECRET TO PERFECTING PASTRY

Pastry is called pastry because it evolved from a flour and water paste that was applied to meat before roasting to seal in the juices. It was inedible and would be discarded before serving.

When baking choux pastry, splash a handful of water on the tray just before it goes in the oven. This will provide just enough steam to help the choux rise.

If overkneaded or over-rolled, pastry will shrink. Once mixed, allow it to rest in the fridge or the freezer for half an hour, then when rolled put it back for another half hour before baking.

When kneading pastry, keep hands cold by plunging them into ice water. It will stop the pastry warming up and softening, then stretching when rolled, and then shrinking back in the oven. 🖫

THE SECRETS OF USING A FAN

There is plenty of documentary evidence to show that a Victorian flower code existed, but exactly how formal a fan code there was is open to debate. Some commentators speculate that the "language of fans" was in reality merely an extension of the attitude of a lady toward her would-be suitor. Hence she might flutter her fan flirtatiously, waft it laconically, or even snap it shut in a clear, dismissive "let that be an end to the matter" gesture. Others maintain that it was a much more formal business: that the speed with which the lady used her fan was highly significant, denoting anger, frustration, even love.

Those who take this view to its most extreme believe the language was very specific indeed. The following are a few of the messages that they claim were conveyed:

Resting the fan on the right cheek *yes*	Twirling the fan with the left hand *we are being watched*
Resting the fan on the left cheek *no*	Carrying the fan in front of the face with the right hand *follow me* ⏳

DOUBLE SECRET AGENT REVEALED

In the last years of the Cold War, Aldrich Ames was probably the most successful Soviet agent within the U.S. He worked in counter-espionage at the CIA, but from 1985 was also a double agent and betrayed much of the American intelligence operation within the U.S.S.R. At least ten Russian agents were executed on his information, including Dmitri Polyakov, who had spied for the U.S. since the early 1960s. Ames's motive was financial rather than ideological and he received nearly $3 million for his efforts. He lived at 2512 N. Randolph Street, in Arlington, and would communicate with his Russian handlers by placing chalk marks on a mailbox at 37th and R Streets. ✍

ROSEBUD'S SECRET IDENTITY

Orson Welles's 1941 classic *Citizen Kane* is regularly voted the greatest film ever made. It was Welles's first film, but the 25-year-old had gone to Hollywood intending to make a film of Joseph Conrad's *Heart Of Darkness*, the novella which, 38 years later, Francis Ford Coppola used as the basis for *Apocalypse Now*.

From the very beginning, the references to "Rosebud" baffled viewers. It was the very first word uttered in the film, and is used repeatedly to try and unravel the enigma of the film's central character, the media mogul Charles Foster Kane (based on the real-life tycoon William Randolph Hearst). The film's last line confirms the enigma: "I guess Rosebud is just a piece in a jigsaw puzzle, a missing piece."

For years, film historians and critics battled over the symbolism of "Rosebud." There was even one scurrilous suggestion that Welles had somehow discovered Hearst's pet-name for his mistress's hidden charms. Over the years, Welles deftly stoked the fire of the mystery, although he was quite explicit at the time of the film's opening: "Rosebud is the trade name of a cheap sled on which Kane was playing on the day he was taken away from his home and his mother. In his subconscious it represented the simplicity, the comfort, above all the lack of responsibility in his home, and also it stood for his mother's love, which Kane never lost." 🔔

THE SECRET OF MAKING A GOOD FIRST IMPRESSION

There is a secret to making a good first impression that has nothing to do with your personality, appearance, or natural ability to charm. The single most important factor is to focus on the other person then incorporate the following four elements into the interaction.

First, make them feel liked and appreciated by directly or indirectly showing you understand and respect them.

You could say, for example: "What an interesting idea, I've never thought of it that way before . . ."

Second, establish rapport by showing you have shared interests or areas of connection with them. For example, "Oh yes, I loved that book too, and especially the character of . . ."

Third, stimulate their curiosity and interest by giving them some new and relevant information. For example, to your hairdresser: "I was reading yesterday about Voodoo queen Mary Laveau, did you know she started out cutting the hair of the aristocracy . . ."

Fourth, lighten other people's mood by being playful and humorous. Never walk into a meeting and complain about your terrible journey, or how bad you feel. Stay positive: You don't need to be a comedian, just ratchet your style up a little.

By following these four secret rules, you will have fulfilled all the needs of the other person, which is what first impressions are actually all about. ᕙ

THE SECRET OF EXISTENCE

"FOR BELIEVE ME: THE SECRET FOR HARVESTING FROM EXISTENCE THE GREATEST FRUITFULNESS AND GREATEST ENJOYMENT IS—TO LIVE DANGEROUSLY."
Friedrich Nietzsche (*19th-century German philosopher*)

AUTHORS

LLOYD BRADLEY

THOMAS EATON

EMMA HOOLEY

PATRICK HUMPHRIES

CHARLOTTE WILLIAMSON